S0-AIH-202

When getting Along Seems IMPOSSIBLE

H. NEWTON MALONY

When getting Along Seems IMPOSSIBLE

Fleming H. Revell Company
Old Tappan, New Jersey

Unless otherwise identified, the Scripture quotations in this book are from the Revised Standard Version of the Bible, Copyrighted © 1946, 1952, 1971, by the Division of Christian Education of the National Council of the Churches of Christ in the United States of America, and are used by permission. All rights reserved.

Scripture quotations identified TEV are from the *Good News Bible* — Old Testament: Copyright © American Bible Society 1976: New Testament: Copyright © American Bible Society 1966, 1971, 1976.

Scripture quotations identified KJV are from the King James Version of the Bible.

Excerpts from "Everybody Needs Somebody That They Can Talk To," by John Prine, are copyright © 1971 Cotillion Music, Inc./Sour Grapes Music, Inc. Used by permission. All rights reserved.

Library of Congress Cataloging-in-Publication Data

Malony, H. Newton.
    When getting along seems impossible/H. Newton Malony.
       p. cm.
    ISBN 0-8007-1629-9
    1. Interpersonal relations—Religious aspects—Christianity.
2. Conflict management—Religious aspects—Christianity.   I. Title.
BV4509.5.M264 1989   89-34080
248.4—dc20   CIP

All rights reserved. No part of this publication may be reproduced, stored in a retrieval system, or transmitted in any form or by any means — electronic, mechanical, photocopy, recording, or any other — except for brief quotations in printed reviews, without the prior permission of the publisher.

Copyright © 1989 by H. Newton Malony
Published by the Fleming H. Revell Company
Old Tappan, New Jersey 07675
Printed in the United States of America

To all those, like myself,
who find it hard to remain Christian
when the going gets rough.

Contents

Part III: The Conventional Way

Part IV: The Christian Way

Part V: Practical Conflict Reduction

Foreword

There is nothing that gives me more pain than conflict; and there are few things I am poorer at avoiding. Conflict sneaks up behind me and wallops me when I am not looking for it. I get into it when I want nothing more than to avoid it. And once in it, I want nothing more than to get out of it. Conflict leaves me unsettled. It robs me of joy. I hate it with all my heart. I am a charter member of the "Conflict Haters of the World."

Everything in me cries for peace. I know that life will never be a mush of tranquil serenity. Not for any of us. But can we not at least reduce our conflict? Avoid at least some it? And heal it when we cannot get around it?

Anyone who reads Newton Malony's wise and engaging book will discover practical ways to turn the inevitable conflicts of life into opportunities for peace.

Malony's book taught me many things. But the one that did me the most good was the truth that the conflicts we have with other people rise from conflicts within ourselves. He also taught me that the route to peace with angry people runs straight through our own hearts. Again, the age-old biblical truth breaks out as the most practical wisdom: "Where do these wars and battles between yourselves first start? Isn't it precisely in the desires fighting inside your own selves?" Settle the conflicts in my heart and I have the key to happy relationships with other people. A good beginning!

I have more than once thought that I was in conflict with someone about something, when I was really in conflict with myself. I was in a conflict because I feared that my own self-esteem was attacked. My own sense of worth. My own feelings of self-respect. And my own ego was in jeopardy because I did not have inner peace. So when someone came along and did something to expose my lack of inner resources, I rose up in anxious self-defense. Yet, all the while, I believed I was fighting for some cause or some grand principle. My conflict outside began with a conflict inside. Malony understands the inner roots of outer conflict, the self-generated flame that ignites conflicts with other people.

This is only one explanation for Malony's success. It happens to be the most important to me. When in conflict, look for the real source. The source may be you. Deal with the source, and you have the beginnings of a peace that ornery, mean, or just competitive people around you cannot disturb.

Another gift that comes with Malony's book is hope. Newton Malony nourishes us in hope. He looks at our conflicts from two vantage points. He writes as a person of hope for ultimate peace, for the breaking out of shalom in all the world among all the races and nations of humankind. But he also writes as a specialist who has the knowledge and the skills to bring the healing powers of shalom into the agonies of our present conflicts. This is a great gift, and he shares it through real life stories drawn from his rich experience in helping people to learn how to avoid conflict and to resolve it when they get themselves into it.

In this remarkable book, Malony blends faith with knowledge and skill with wisdom. He synthesizes trained know-how with gifted insight, mastered technique with spiritual sensitivity, psychotherapy with tender ministry. It is what I would have expected from this wise and loving colleague, but still, as I read the book, I felt as if I had been given a gift I would not have anticipated.

Malony is a realist. He knows that there is no life without conflict. He knows that life would be drab and dull if it were all a becalmed sea of tranquility. And he knows that we are expecting too much in a broken and fallen world if we expect perfect *shalom* here and now. He is a realist, but he also knows that we have more conflict than we need to have and that our conflicts bring us more misery than we need to feel. He is a helpful, healing, and hopeful realist.

What he gives us is not the illusive promise of untroubled life on a placid plane of problemless peace. He gives us instead the practical help of a proven and artful therapist for reducing our pain-racked conflicts, for avoiding needless conflicts, and for resolving the conflicts we cannot avoid.

Every now and then a book comes on the scene that tells us what we already dimly know, reminds us of what we want with all our hearts, and then shows us, in ways we can all understand, how to reduce our pain and increase the peace that is our hearts' desire. This is such a book. It is a gift.

Lewis B. Smedes
Sierra Madre, California
1989

When
Getting Along
Seems
IMPOSSIBLE

Part I
Conflict

1

Tommy's Neighborhood Rampage

or

What Is Conflict?

The soldier is only nineteen — far too young to be sweating his way through the jungle, watching his every step, barely daring to breathe. Suddenly, an indistinct shape moves in the tangle of green off to his left and he fires into the undergrowth, aware that he will die if his reactions are just a little too slow that day.

Across the world, a young mother stands in her kitchen, the telephone gripped in her hand, listening to another mother complain, ever so politely, about little Tommy. Tommy has just ransacked the neighborhood, and she is hearing the implied message that she's a bad mother. As her face turns beet red, she takes a deep breath and snaps, "Oh? And I suppose your son's an angel? Listen, you. . . ."

Which of the two is in conflict?

Both are. Conflict is a fight for life, whether it takes place on a formal or informal battlefield. Sometimes it's an obvious choice of physically killing or being killed, but often in life we find our self-esteem suffering such a serious blow that we are forced to defend ourselves or be psychologically devastated. The psychological danger the young mother was facing was just as real as the indistinct shape in the soldier's jungle, and both the soldier and the mother were overwhelmed by desperate feelings that led to drastic action. Both were in conflict, fighting for their lives.

The Bible provides us with a classic example of conflict in the story of Saul and David. After David bravely volunteered to fight Goliath and defeated him, Saul brought David into his court, making him a captain over his soldiers in the war against the Philistines. "And David went out whithersoever Saul sent him, and behaved himself wisely. . . and he was accepted in the sight of all the people. . ." (1 Samuel 18:5 KJV). The people of Israel were so happy with David's victories over the Philistines that the women came out to meet Saul and David after a battle, dancing and singing with joy, ". . . Saul hath slain his thousands, and David his ten thousands" (1 Samuel 18:7 KJV).

It's doubtful that there was any snub or insult intended in the women's song. It was just a song of joy — good poetry sung to please two heroes. But Saul took it wrong, and it deeply hurt his self-esteem. Perhaps he had a literal mind and couldn't laugh off a song hinting that young David was ten times the man he was. To him, the women's song was an indication that David was loved more than he was, "and Saul eyed David from that day and forward" (1 Samuel 18:9 KJV).

We've all seen jealous people squinting their eyes, tilting their heads, and looking for evidence that what they fear most is true: that they are not liked as well as someone else. When the jealous person is a powerful king, the object of his jealousy had better tread lightly and mind his manners!

As time went by, David became even more successful in battle. His fame grew even greater, and then Saul suffered another loss at the hands of the young man. His daughter fell in love with David. The boy was taking all the glory — taking the love of his own daughter — what next? The kingdom? Saul was becoming desperately afraid that David had designs on his throne. The young man was certainly popular and strong enough to overthrow Saul anytime he wanted. Several times, in fits of rage, Saul actually hurled a spear at David, hoping to pin him to the wall and end the mental agony he was suffering. Finally, certain that his suspicions were correct, Saul ordered David killed, forcing him to flee for his life.

Notice how desperate Saul had become. He certainly had other options available to him besides killing David. He could have ordered the boy back to his flocks, thereby removing him from the public eye and letting him fade into a dim memory in the minds of the people. He could have fabricated a scandal or insulted David publicly, both of which would have diminished David's popularity. But, because he was in such extreme mental agony, Saul went for the ultimate satisfaction — death. Saul was truly a man in conflict!

It's important to note, however, that David was *not* in conflict. No matter what Saul did or said, David remained calm, even refusing to kill Saul when he had the opportunity. David felt no threat to his self-esteem and was confident that he could protect himself from Saul's army. He felt no need for drastic action. Through it all, although he was fleeing for his life, David never went into conflict.

The story of Saul and David provides us with a definition of *conflict:* a desperate state of mind in which people feel their self-esteem is so endangered that something desperate must be done to retore it. Our nineteen-year-old soldier had to kill or be killed; the young mother could not hear herself accused of being a bad mother without lashing out to restore her self-respect. Both were as much in conflict as Saul, chasing David through the wilderness.

Conflict Is Internal

Since conflicts are actually feelings and thoughts, they obviously exist inside us and are not objective, tangible entities. This explains why David never went into conflict, no matter what Saul did. David's only goal was to serve his king. He wasn't trying to take away Saul's throne, and he was genuinely surprised by Saul's actions. The conflict existed in Saul's mind — as conflicts exist *inside* people, not *between* them.

Many people, if put into David's position, would go into conflict as a protective measure. Many would have killed Saul or taken the throne in retaliation, but David was made of stronger stuff than most. He kept calm, kept sight of his goals, and never went into conflict.

This is hard for us to understand because we normally think of conflict as being a problem between people, not an internal, individual response to a given situation. Some people define conflict as two or more objects trying to occupy the same space at the same time. Douglass Lewis, author of *Resolving Church Conflict*, gave the following example of this definition of conflict:

> When my daughter Laura was five, she loved to play with cardboard boxes. A big box would occupy her for hours. She would crawl into it, sit inside it, or hide under it. One day, when a friend came to play, their activity centered around a modest-sized box. After watching Laura sit in the box, Josh naturally wanted to get in as well. He gave Laura a shove and she reciprocated. A shoving match followed. Soon they were hitting each other, screaming, and crying.

In this situation, some people would say the box was the source of conflict, even though the fault was not in the box but in the feelings each child had about the box. Both Josh and Laura felt their wishes were being ignored. Both felt they would lose self-respect if they didn't fight for their rights. Boxes only become conflicts when children feel they have to control them or lose self-respect. Thrones only become conflicts if a king feels another man is a threat to his self-respect.

Most of us would agree that Saul wasn't thinking clearly, that he was worrying unnecessarily, but that's exactly the point: These feelings, no matter how unreasonable, were real to Saul and determined his actions. The jealousy he felt over David's popularity became distressful to him. He had gone into conflict.

James Alan McPherson wrote "The Story of a Scar," which is a modern illustration of how people go into conflict. A woman with a horrible scar recounts the story of her injury to another patient as they wait in a plastic surgeon's office. She had begun to date a fellow postal worker who became unreasonably jealous when she was transferred to the night shift. He thought she no longer liked him, while in fact, she still adored him. He became very suspicious and demanding. Early one morning, as the night workers were relaxing in the lounge after work, her boyfriend appeared. He said to her, "It's time for you to go home." Her friends protested, telling him not to be so bossy, but he insisted. When his girlfriend refused to go with him, the man took out his knife and slashed her face, causing the terrible scar that brought her to the plastic surgeon's office.

This man's conflict was internal. His self-esteem was so threatened by his girlfriend's refusal to leave with him that desperate emotions led him to the drastic action of scarring the woman he loved.

Conflict is not an objective fact; it is a subjective experience, a person's state of mind. Conflicts cannot be seen, touched, smelled, or heard — although they are very real to the person experiencing them.

Of course, Saul and the postal worker's boyfriend are extreme examples of conflict. Most often, conflict leads us to hurt people verbally or socially rather than physically. Whenever we see people shouting at each other, calling names, or attempting to defame each other, we can be sure they are in conflict. They feel their self-esteem is in danger, and they use destructive action to restore their sense of worth.

Major-league baseball pitcher Rick Sutcliff shouted at manager Tommy Lasorda and threw furniture around the office when he was not included in the Los Angeles Dodger lineup for the playoffs several years ago. It seemed to me that he must have felt that his self-esteem was deeply threatened. He was in conflict. When a receptionist becomes sullen and refuses to speak to her coworkers after being reprimanded for being late to work we know that her pride has been hurt and she is in conflict. When a boss says to a subordinate, "I am the boss. What I say goes. Do it the way I say or you're fired," he is in conflict. When a husband hits his wife; when a child runs away; when a colleague refuses to speak to you — they are in conflict.

Self-Esteem

Our self-esteem is very important to us, or we wouldn't go to such lengths to protect it. The young mother who snapped at her neighbor will have to spend weeks patching up that relationship. She will be embarrassed by her harsh words and wish she had thought before speaking. But at the time, restoring her self-esteem as a mother was important, and she only did what she felt she had to do at that moment.

What is self-esteem? Why is it so important to us? Self-esteem is simply the opinion we come to have of ourselves. We aren't born with it; we acquire it as we grow and interact with others. It doesn't take a tiny baby long to learn that his cries receive immediate attention while his smiles bring smiles in return. Even a toddler knows that if she asks her parents for a special toy, she will get it if at all possible. Every positive parental response tells children that they are loved for themselves, that they are *worthy* of being loved. By the time most children start school, they have acquired a good amount of positive self-esteem. They basically like themselves, are proud of who they are, feel good about their roles in life, and feel loved and supported at home. Because they basically like themselves, children are often surprised and affronted when things don't go their way in life. Fairness is very important to a child, and anything that damages a child's self-esteem is definitely unfair!

We all work hard to protect and increase the good feelings we have developed about ourselves since childhood. Laura and Josh were not actually fighting over the cardboard box, but were defending their self-esteem, their right to have their feelings considered in a social situation. If an adult had found a way for both to maintain their self-esteem — perhaps by finding a second box or arbitrating a mutually satisfactory sharing arrangement — the two would not have had to fight. If the complaining mother on the telephone had not implied the other mother was a "bad" mother, the second mother would not have retaliated to protect her self-esteem. If the young soldier had not feared losing his life — the ultimate loss of self-esteem — he would not have fired blindly into the jungle. If Saul had not feared losing his popularity, he would not have threatened the life of David.

As you can see from these examples, our self-esteem is made up of more than one component. Laura, Josh, and the young mother were fighting for status; the young soldier was fighting for his identity. Both identity and status are components of self-esteem, and loss of them will throw a person into conflict.

Identity

We identify ourselves through the various roles we play in our lives. If someone asks, "Who are you?", our first reply will likely list our name and some of the things we do: mother, father, doctor, teacher, and so forth. Like actors, we each play many roles in life, all of which are part of who we are —how we see and identify ourselves. We are the roles we play.

The main thing to remember about these various roles is that we act them out in relation to other people. They are not solo performances: Teachers need students, nurses need patients, mothers need children, and salesmen need customers. Thus, our roles in life are highly social and only make sense when they're part of a relationship. We depend on others to interact with us, and having a role to play means we have a social identity that is dependent on other people.

To have an identity, we have to fit into one or more of the roles our society recognizes. As psychologist Erik Erickson notes, you can't be an Indian chief in cultures that have no Indians. There are only a limited number of roles available, and you can't write your own brand-new part in life that no one recognizes. Others have to recognize your role and give you the title or you cannot be known as the butcher, the baker, or the candlestick maker, as the nursery rhyme says.

People with self-esteem have identified roles they play in relationship to others. One of the major parts of our identity revolves around our work — the roles we've achieved through effort and training. However, our identity is also composed of roles that have been ascribed or given to us: son, mother, American. Some roles we work for and some are given to us.

Although achieved roles are an important part of our identity, they are vulnerable to outside forces, and losing them deeply threatens our self-esteem. When the market changes, when automation does away with a position, when people quit or are fired from their jobs, their self-esteem takes a serious blow because part of their identity has suddenly been taken away. This was Saul's problem; he felt that David threatened his identity as a king. This is a problem for many people who have built their identities around their jobs. Who are they when they reach sixty-five and find themselves walking a beach in Florida? How can a vice-president be a vice-president without a company? A sudden loss of achieved identity can seriously diminish a person's self-esteem and throw him into conflict.

Fortunately, most of us know we are more than our jobs, and some parts of our identities cannot be taken away. Mothers will always be mothers, brothers will always be brothers, and these roles help us weather the storm when our achieved roles are threatened. However, even ascribed identities are vulnerable. An American can move to another country, cease to be a legal American, and feel a loss of self-esteem because he no longer has a role as an American. A father could get drunk and abuse his family or a spouse could be unfaithful and lose his wife. When these things affect our ascribed roles, our self-esteem is in danger.

Status

The second part of self-esteem is status, or reputation. When we say, "Sue has a good reputation," we mean she has high status, is appreciated, and valued as a person. Those with high status have power: They are listened to, courted, and followed. Those with low status are discounted, avoided, and ignored. Remember your high school years, with their socially powerful "in" and "out" groups?

Status, like identity, depends on relationships. A reputation is always a matter of how we are seen by *others*, not how we would like to be seen. One sociologist suggests that status is like a "looking glass self." Our status is dependent on what we think others see when they look at us. So we look in the looking glass and try to imagine what others are thinking about us when we're together. Like it or not, to some extent we are who we think others think we are. We value ourselves as we think we are valued by others.

Of course we never really know what others think of us, but we vigilantly try to assess their opinions, using our psychological antennas to discover what's in their minds. We are like weathermen who constantly try to determine what the weather is like around us.

Therefore, our self-esteem is based on who we are (identity) and our reputation (status). It's quite possible to have a firm identity and low status or to have high status and no identity, but most of us strive to attain a firm identity and high status during our lifetime.

As an example of how a person could have a firm identity and low status, take the case of a professor at Harvard who gets a dismal rating from his students in the student-run annual *Red Book*. All the professors have firm identities, but one who pulls a bad rating in the book has very low status.

People can also have high status and no identity. Many retired businessmen and women have high status in the community and church, even though they are no longer associated with the jobs that formed a major part of their identities.

When Does the Conflict Balloon Go Up?

If conflict arises in a person when his or her self-esteem is endangered, at what point does this happen?

How much identity can you lose before you feel conflict? How much status?

Because of the wide variation in personalities, there is no fixed point at which everyone goes into conflict. Some people are more laid-back and confident than others.

It can be safely assumed that if a person's identity and status are uncertain or threatened, he or she will go into conflict. However, status and identity are not always equally important to a person. If a woman plays multiple roles and enjoys them all, she doesn't need to play them all perfectly. If she is a musician, nurse, mother, ballroom dancer, and choir member, the fact that she'll never be a great violinist won't threaten her self-esteem.

In contrast, a person's status may outweigh the fact that he's not a great success on the job. Friendly, supportive, beloved teachers may never lose an ounce of self-respect over the fact that they aren't the head of their departments or that they have not read the latest research in their fields.

Everyone strikes his own balance between the value of identity and status, but no one else knows where that balance is struck. How often have you heard someone say, "I didn't know it mattered that much to you"? We can never really know what people think and feel about themselves, but we do know that self-esteem is extremely important to us all, and we all feel conflict when it is threatened.

During World War II, the army tried to find a way to determine what type of soldier would do well in Alaska. They ran extensive tests before deciding that the best predicator of adjustment was to ask the simple question, "Do you want to go to Alaska?" Those who didn't want to go couldn't adjust; those who did adjusted just fine. Sometimes you just have to ask the right question, even if it does seem too simple to work. The best question to ask about conflict is, "Are you in conflict?"

2

Sailing to Catalina

or

The Differences Between Problems and Conflicts

To properly understand conflict, we have to keep in mind that it is an inner state of mind, not the obstacles we run into in the course of our daily lives. Conflicts only exist in our hearts and minds. But, that leaves us with a predicament. What do we call those situations we might normally label conflicts? For example, if hearing about little Tommy ransacking the neighborhood wasn't a conflict, what was it?

The best term to use for a situation like this is *problem*. When two people try to occupy the same space, they have a problem. When a boy runs into a neighbor's rosebush while chasing a baseball, there is a problem. Problems arise quite often when autonomous people interact. Because we are all independent and free, we all see the world differently and tend to do things differently. Problems between people are to be expected in life unless you're a hermit, and even hermits have problems with people who wander too close to their caves.

Go back and consider the two mothers on the telephone. When the conversation began, they had a minor problem. Little Tommy had just done something socially unacceptable, and his mother had to be informed of it. Most mothers want to know these things, and at first our young mother was probably glad her neighbor had called. If things had gone well, she would have thanked the other mother for calling and taken steps to correct the problem by controlling Tommy. But the problem escalated. The two mothers saw the situation differently, and somewhere along the line the caller implied that Tommy's mother was not bringing her child up properly. This created a more serious problem, but it was one that still could have been ignored or discussed and resolved.

Implying the neighbor was a bad mother was a tremendous blow to her self-esteem — one this particular mother could not accept. She had a violent emotional reaction to the implication and lashed out verbally to protect her self-esteem. In this case, the problem caused a conflict in her mind and resulted in drastic action she'll regret as soon as she hangs up the phone and deals with Tommy.

Another mother in the same situation might not have gone into conflict at all. She might have realized the caller was overreacting, admitted Tommy was a terror, or been able to absorb the blow to her self-esteem without damage. In that case, there would have been no conflict within her, and the problem would have remained little Tommy, the monster.

It's important to reserve the term *conflict* for what goes on inside our heads and to apply the term *problem* to those situations involving disputes or differences of opinion. Of course situations themselves can sometimes be overwhelming, but until they threaten our self-esteem, they remain problems we can solve, rather than conflicts to be overcome. Viktor Frankl's experience in a concentration camp is a good example of this differentiation. His will to live and find meaning in his situation shows how he turned this most serious and devastating situation into a problem he could handle through thought and logic.

The fact that even threatening situations can be considered problems was clearly illustrated in the movie *Cool Hand Luke*. Luke (Paul Newman) was a provocative, resistant member of a prison chain gang. He and his fellow prisoners were worked hard, fed poorly, and constantly harassed. Luke never quite cooperated with the system, and after one particularly obstinate act of behavior, the prison commander told the assembled prisoners, "What we have here is a failure to communicate." He then solved his problem by locking Luke in a small hut called "the box." Even though our sympathy lies with Luke, we have to admit the commander was right in his terminology. He had a *problem* with Luke, not a conflict. Neither he nor Luke ever went into conflict — both stayed cool and dealt with their problems in their own way.

Most of us intuitively recognize the difference between problems and conflicts, even if we've never really thought about it. We know that if a particular situation frustrates or stresses us, it may become a catalyst capable of sending us into conflict. We all have our own personal weaknesses and pet peeves. Say the neighbor's dog regularly comes over and rampages through your carefully tended flower garden. In every other way, the dog is a good dog. Your children love him, he loves them, and even you feel a certain amount of affection for him. But, if he makes a move toward that flower garden, the chances are pretty good that you'll go into conflict, especially if you have a good deal of pride invested in the garden. Until he makes his move toward the roses, the dog is just a potential problem. Once he sets foot on the garden's border, he is a problem. When he starts digging up the irises, then he causes you to go into conflict. On the other hand, if you planned to divide those irises that day, you won't mind the dog helping you dig them up, and you may not go into conflict at all. No matter what he does, the dog's visit can be no more than a problem; the conflict is inside you as you react to his actions.

Success, Stress, and Distress

Imagine that we have decided to sail a thirty-seven-foot boat from San Pedro, California, to Catalina Island for the weekend, which is about a twenty-mile trip. We gather at the dock early Saturday morning and prepare the boat for the trip. We stock up with plenty of food, drink, and gas for the trolling motor. We check the sails and the condition of the hull, and soon we are ready to go.

It's a beautiful day, and the weather report suggests there is only a slight chance of a storm. Since these storms usually pass over this area, and because the sun is shining and the sea is gentle, we decide to embark as soon as possible. The breeze is from the north at a moderate speed. After we clear the breakwater, the wind shifts a bit and blows us toward our destination with only a shift of the sails. It is an absolutely marvelous day for sailing, and we sit back and let the boat ride the gentle swells in a majestic manner. We chat and snack in relaxed comfort.

About halfway there, an unexpected storm comes in from the north. The wind shifts, and we are blown a bit off course. It's difficult to hold the boat on course; we can see the island, but we are being carried past it. We tack the sails. One of us positions herself on the bow and gives directions when we stray off course. It takes all of us working together to plow through the storm, but some time later the wind subsides, the rain stops, the waves settle down, and the sun comes out. We sit back and relax again.

Just as we are about to enter Catalina harbor, an unexpected event occurs; we hit a submerged object. The boat shakes and stops dead in the water. One of us runs up front to see what we hit, another rushes below to check for damage. We see nothing in the water, but there is a hole in the bottom of the boat, and water is pouring in. We are in danger of sinking. It's still too far to swim to shore, and we're in deep water. We all rush down and push clothing, mattresses, and boards into the hole, bailing frantically. Now it matters little where we came from or where we are going; we only want to stay afloat. Our very survival is at stake.

Finally we stop the leak. We come back up on deck and look at one another. Catalina is still in view, but we have forgotten our plans for the weekend. We are just glad to have survived. Soon we regain our composure and start off again for the island.

This fanciful journey illustrates the differences between problems and conflicts. It also depicts a third type of situation, in which neither problems nor conflicts exist.

When we first started out on our sail, the weather was beautiful and we faced no difficulties. We were in what could be called a *success condition*. We enjoy lots of days like this in life, days with no frustrations, no disagreements. The sacrifices we do have to make on success days aren't burdensome because we can see they are helping us reach our goals, and people are cooperating with us. On days like this, we wake up happy and go to bed happy, hoping the next day will be just as kind to us.

Then a storm comes along and we can't sit back and relax any longer. We have to assess the situation and make adjustments to keep our lives on course. But we're generally pretty good sailors who know how to ride out a storm. Even though we're not relaxed, we remain calm and confident. Days like these are *stress conditions*. Where once there was agreement, someone raises an objection or fails to do his job, producing a problem. Usually, we remain calm and use our logic and skill to work through the difficulties. Then we can go back to enjoying our success days.

The third situation we run into in life is the *distress situation*. When we hit the submerged object and tore a hole in the boat, we had no choice but to drop everything and put all our efforts into survival. Even getting to Catalina Island didn't matter anymore — our only goal was saving our lives. Conflict is a distress situation. Things are totally out of control, our very being feels threatened, and we must take drastic measures to stay alive. Others may see the situation and consider it just a problem that can be solved, but we, because we feel vulnerable, experience it as a matter of life and death. In a situation like this, we go nowhere as far as our life goals are concerned; we're just fighting to stay alive. This is what it's like to go into conflict.

Success, stress, and distress are the three basic life conditions. All our experiences fit into one of these categories. (*See* Experience Diagram.)

Experience Diagram

	Frustration Level	How We Feel	Emotional Result
Success	None	In Control	Achievement
Stress	Moderate	Challenged	Challenge
Distress	Overwhelming	Threatened	Conflict

Wouldn't it be wonderful if all our days were successful ones and we never had to deal with stress or conflict? But that's not the way life is, and if you lined the three conditions up in order, from most typical to least typical, they'd go: stress, success, distress.

We could draw a bar graph representing the amount of time the average person spends in success, stress, and distress. (*See* Stress Bar Graph.)

Stress Bar Graph

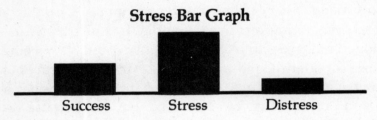

| Success | Stress | Distress |

It's impossible to live without some frustration and stress. We're all created human beings with our own wills, our own goals, our own opinions, and no one gets his way all the time.

The way life is structured also makes stress inevitable. As a teacher, I always begin a term hoping that all my students will love me and think I'm the perfect teacher. I know this won't happen, but that doesn't prevent me from being shocked when I read the student evaluations at the end of the term and discover not everyone liked me. I always succeed with some and fail with others, but I've never taught a class where there was complete harmony or success. People are different, and it's inevitable that they'll see things from their own individual, idiosyncratic points of view. The stress of knowing I am not completely successful with every student is inevitable.

Although there's no way to escape stress and problems in life, it is theoretically possible to live a life without distress — without going into conflict. It's not structurally necessary for people to feel their self-esteem so threatened that they go into conflict. However, conflict seems to come to us all.

I was driving through an affluent section of town one day with a friend who is a counselor. Looking at the golf course and majestic homes we were passing, I remarked, "I bet those homes house many happy families."

"You know better than that," my friend replied. "I've counseled many people from around here."

He was right; I did know better. Rich people suffer threats and distress in life too, although their money may lessen the number of times they go into conflict.

This fact was proven to me several years ago. I had been teaching conflict management for some time and knew all the definitions we have been discussing here, plus several ways of handling conflict. I, of all people, should have known enough to stay out of conflict. Yet when a colleague of mine agreed to take on one of my graduate students after we had been working together on a project for two years, I went into conflict. I was angry and bitter toward this colleague; I brooded over the situation, indulged in gossip about her, and hoped she would lose her job. The issue of the graduate student was no longer the issue between us. The issue was my pride and self-esteem. I felt deeply threatened, and my behavior was a drastic attempt to regain a sense of self-worth. I represent all those people who think they'll never go into conflict because they're too educated, too wise, or too rich to experience distress. But they still do, because although conflict isn't necessary, it does seem inevitable.

Solve Problems, Reduce Conflict

Most of us spend a good percentage of our time working through life's stresses. Murphy's Law — "Anything that can go wrong, will" — is the rule, not the exception, in life.

A challenge is one more difference between problems and conflicts that should be noted. Our chart uses the word *challenged* for how we feel in stress situations. Stress is capable of drawing out the best in us as we work to solve our problems; it often makes us into better, more successful people. In contrast, distress makes us feel threatened, alone, and defensive. It overcomes all logic, leaving us dead in the water. This leads to the maxim — solve *problems* but *reduce* conflict.

To illustrate this, let's go back to our trip to Catalina. When the storm arose and we had to adjust our sails to shifts in the wind and use our compass to stay on course, we were in a stress condition. Our chart calls this experience a challenge. We used our sailing skills and mental reasoning to decide what to do, we felt we could meet the challenge, and we solved the problem. That's what is supposed to happen when we're under stress.

When we hit the submerged object, we became distressed and put all our effort into staying afloat. While we were busy staying alive, we made no progress toward Catalina. Before we even cared about going anywhere, we had to reduce the threat to our survival.

When I go into conflict, I stop solving problems and work entirely off my emotions to reduce the threat to my self-esteem. I don't care about any of my life goals anymore; all I care about is reducing my conflict by whatever means are available. Until my feelings of danger, helplessness, and panic are reduced to a manageable level, I will be unreasonable and unable to solve any of my problems. "Reduce stress — solve problems" is a fact of life, not just a nice saying.

3

Rousing the Sleeping Giant
or
How Conflict Arises

Conflict is like a sleeping giant who awakens and terrorizes the nearby village from time to time. Most of the time, the villagers go about their daily lives in peace, sometimes for years, but every so often, without much warning, the giant stumbles out of his cave, tramples the crops, scares the stock away, and generally devastates the innocent villagers.

Now, the villagers aren't stupid, and their best minds have been trying for generations to figure out what awakens the giant. He doesn't come out on any regular schedule, they keep away from his cave all the time, and they even leave vast quantities of his favorite food between the village and his cave. Nothing seems to keep him asleep forever, or keep him from walking over their houses when he does stir.

Conflict works the same way. We keep asking ourselves, "What causes conflict to emerge? What frightens us so much that we feel we must fight for our lives?" Most of the time, we see frustrations and problems as challenges to meet through problem solving, not as overwhelming dangers to our self-esteem. But, now and then the giant awakens, tramples all over our logic, and goes on an emotional rampage. If only we knew when this was going to happen!

In *QB VII*, Leon Uris tells the story of two people caught in a frustrating situation. One of them goes into conflict, but the other doesn't. This story illustrates the dilemma we face when we try to understand the factors that provoke conflict.

In *QB VII*, physician Adam Kelno was accused by Jewish authorities of engaging in human genetic experimentation in a Polish concentration camp during World War II. His involvement was almost unbelievable because he was not apprehended at the time and had become a respected physician in England after the war. Kelno had spent a number of years serving the natives in an isolated hospital in the South Pacific and was heavily involved in service to the poor in London. He denied any involvement in such experiments, although he did admit that he served on the medical staff at Jadwiga, the prison camp where he served the needs of the prisoners under very trying circumstances. He filed suit against both Israel and the London newspapers for libel and slander when they accused him of complicity.

The slander trial progressed and appeared to be headed toward the exoneration of Dr. Kelno until the defense produced a surprise witness who completely changed the situation. Dr. Maria Viskova was a Polish physician who had also been at Jadwiga. She had served as a doctor alongside Adam Kelno. She confirmed the fact that genetic experimentation was done at Jadwiga under orders from Germany. She denied that she participated, but attested to the fact that Adam Kelno was heavily involved in the research.

At this point Kelno changed his testimony. He admitted his involvement but insisted that he did what he did under duress. He had been told to cooperate or die.

Dr. Viskova was recalled to the stand and asked if what Dr. Kelno had said was true. She confirmed that she too had been threatened with loss of her life if she did not help with the experiments. "Then, how was it that you survived?" she was asked.

"I told them I would not help under any circumstances," she replied. "If they wanted to kill me, I told them to go right ahead, but I would not experiment on human beings." They did not kill her, and she went on serving the needs of the prisoners.

This is a dramatic illustration of how one person may go into conflict while another doesn't under the identical circumstances. Adam Kelno so feared for his life that he engaged in the drastic behavior of human experimentation. Maria Viskova, although threatened in the same manner, did not go into conflict. Even though the situation was catastrophic, she was not overwhelmed. Her self-esteem remained intact and she did not engage in drastic behavior.

What can we learn about the rise of conflict from this illustration?

One or Another

The first principle that helps us to understand when conflict will arise is the *one or another* rule. This rule states that certain issues are more important to some people than to others. We know this by experience when we see people blow up over issues that don't bother us at all. We may have sympathy for their point and even agree with them intellectually, but our emotions aren't as strong or we don't see the issue as all that vital to our own lives.

Kelno and Viskova saw their problems differently. Their common problem was the danger to their lives: cooperate or die. It's tempting to say that Kelno was more concerned with saving his life than Viskova was, but it's doubtful that this is true. People don't take life lightly, and Viskova undoubtedly wanted to live as much as Kelno did. The difference was that Viskova kept her head and saw beyond the question of life and death, then decided that life was not worth living if she had to violate her medical ethics to stay alive. Kelno, on the other hand, decided that medical ethics weren't worth dying for.

Although we may admire Viskova and disapprove of Kelno's choice, the observation that there are differences in people's choices is made without prejudice. People do have different priorities; certain issues are more significant to some people than to others. In this particular example, the loss of physical life was more threatening to Kelno than to Viskova. He engaged in drastic action because he went into conflict. Viskova did not become distressed to that degree.

In other words, conflict emerges over different issues in different people. When forced to choose between one or another, do or die, people will choose and react differently. Some will calmly make the choice necessary and live or die with its consequences; others will go into conflict and choose differently.

Few or Many

The second principle that determines whether people go into conflict or not I will call the *few or many* rule. This refers to the fact that some people have very few issues over which they will fight for their lives, while others have many. Psychologists call this ego involvement. Since conflict is the point at which people's self-esteem becomes so threatened that they feel they must engage in drastic behavior to restore their sense of self-worth, those whose egos are tied in with many issues will be in conflict more often than those who are ego involved in only a few things.

Ego involvement should not be confused with interest. People can be interested in many things but still be able to take them or leave them. Their many interests aren't necessarily related to their ego or self-esteem. However, people who are ego involved with many issues are very vulnerable to going into conflict often. The frustration they feel when challenged or resisted penetrates to the very core of their being. They feel that if they do not win or if their opinion is not supported, they will be devastated. Since their self-esteem is tied to so many things, they are constantly in danger of going into conflict. With such people every issue becomes a major issue. They make few distinctions between major and minor issues.

Normally, the amount of time and energy we spend in distress is less than that spent in success or stress conditions. However, the more issues over which we're ego involved, the more time and energy we'll spend in conflict.

Does this mean that ego involvement is to be avoided or is unhealthy? By all means, no. Some of the world's finest accomplishments have come about because of an individual's ego involvement with a cause or project. These are the most dedicated workers in the world, people we can't do without. But they do get hurt because of their dedication. They do go into conflict more often than less-dedicated people and pay a price for their involvement. The more ego involvement, the greater the possibility of threat and distress, and the greater the likelihood of going into conflict. This is a fact that must not be forgotten.

Now and Then

The third principle affecting when the sleeping giant of conflict will emerge is called *now and then*. This means that a given situation may provoke a person to go into conflict on one occasion but not on another. The first two principles discussed — one thing or another, few or many — seem to imply that if we knew which issues and how many issues were related to a person's self-esteem, we might be able to predict when he or she would go into conflict. Like the villagers in our giant story, we could try to find a pattern to the giant's activity. However, the now and then principle makes such predictions unreliable.

The problem is, sometimes we're more vulnerable to distress than other times — even over the same issue. This happens because frustration is cumulative. If we're already under stress, we're more likely to go into conflict, even if we've been able to handle the same problem in the past. We all have good days and bad days, and on a bad day we're more vulnerable to conflict.

The experience of a certain graduate student illustrates this principle. She was very intelligent and competent. These qualities helped her get a graduate assistantship at a prestigious university. Her husband and young daughter moved with her to the university town, where she entered into her studies with relish. She managed her duties well for the first six months. Then in one week's time much of her life came apart. Had the problems not all happened at once, she would have handled them better.

The stock market plunged, and she and her husband lost several thousand dollars. On Tuesday of that week, her daughter came down with a fever and the mother had to miss two classes. On Thursday, a glitch appeared in a computer program and two weeks' worth of data were lost. To top it all off, their car broke down and the repairs would cost several hundred dollars.

Up until Friday night, she was more or less handling the stress. She had lost some sleep during her daughter's illness and had been preoccupied over the loss of her research data, but her husband had been supportive, and she had not broken down or gone into a panic. Then, just as they were trying to find a way to pay for the car repairs, her mother called.

Her relationship with her mother was an issue about which she was very vulnerable. She was ego involved with her mother over her striving for independence. Her mother had disapproved of her marrying and pursuing a graduate degree.

When the mother asked, "When will you be coming home for Christmas? We are expecting you for the family dinner, you know," the graduate student broke down and gave her mother a barrage of hostility.

"You want to know when we're coming? Maybe never! You never approve of the way I do things, anyway. We may just stay here for the holidays. I just don't *care* anymore!"

Her mother was deeply shocked. She had not heard an outburst like this in over four years, because the young woman had learned not to react defensively with her mother. On this night, however, all the other stresses had made her vulnerable. Although no single thing she had faced that week was unmanageable, added together they frustrated her so much she couldn't deal with her mother.

I suspect most of us can identify with this student. We know what it's like to have things pile up on us.

When this happens, issues we would normally approach as manageable problems cause us to go into conflict.

In and Out

The fourth principle, *in and out*, refers to the fact that we can go into conflict and out again over the same situation within the same period of time. In a matter of seconds, we may go into and out of conflict, because conflict doesn't always last a long time.

I once had a flat tire on the way to a church speaking engagement. I panicked, certain that I'd never get to the church on time because I had to change the tire. Luckily my wife was with me, and she knew how my self-esteem was being threatened by the possibility of missing this engagement. Although I was in distress, she wasn't, and she told me, "Calm down. They can begin the service without you. They'll understand."

That was enough to bring me out of conflict and allow me to solve my problem by changing the tire. If I'd fixed the tire and then run out of gas before reaching the church, I would have gone into conflict again, and, I hope, my wife would have calmed me down again.

Often the situation is far more serious than a flat tire and no one's around to calm us down. Sometimes we feel very vulnerable and our self-esteem will ebb and flow without our even realizing it. Looking back on the incident, we may see that we went in and out of conflict over the issue, even though it didn't seem obvious at the time.

I have this problem at faculty meetings. These meetings are very important to me. I'm deeply ego involved with what goes on in faculty meetings because I feel my influence and prestige are constantly tested in the decisions we make. I'm one of the older members of the faculty, near the end of my career, and I want to be respected by my peers. My identity and my status are very vulnerable during faculty meetings.

I find myself being hypervigilant at faculty meetings, watching to see what effect my point of view will have. At times I become red in the face and argue almost violently; other times, I'm reasonable and logical. Looking back, I can see that I went in and out of conflict several times during the meeting. At times, my only hope is that I'll calm down by the time the meeting ends!

We all have this happen to us, usually in our more important relationships where we feel vulnerable and dependent. As an argument with our spouse ebbs and flows over an evening, for example, we first feel distress, then comfort, going back and forth, in and out of distress, now hurt, now loved.

More or Less

The final principle that influences the emergence of conflict is *more or less*. More or less refers to the fact that conflict is not an all-or-nothing experience. Sometimes we will feel more conflict over a situation than at other times. The line that separates stress from distress is a dotted line, not a solid one, and even when we go over the line into distress, our conflict will be worse on some occasions than it will be on others.

This is probably due to the fact that the issues threatening us vary in intensity. We see them all as dangerous to our self-esteem, or we wouldn't be in conflict at all, but some seem more hazardous than others.

One day a pastor friend of mine was politely fired by his church's personnel committee, even though he thought everything was going well. His pride was hurt, especially when he heard that some parishioners were threatening to leave the church unless he was replaced.

He got busy and found himself a job that paid almost twice what he was getting at the church and also gave him the opportunity to go to graduate school. This allowed him to save face by implying to his parishioners that they had actually helped him, not hurt him. On the surface, it seemed he had resolved the stressful experience by handling it as a problem to be solved, not as a source of conflict.

He didn't realize how deeply he had been hurt until several months later, when he suddenly began waking up in a cold sweat after dreaming about being fired. His emotions were in deep turmoil, and he remained in conflict for some time, even though his life seemed changed for the better.

Later in life, the same man suffered another professional rebuff that sent him into conflict. He again took action and solved the problem, but this time, his conflict was resolved more easily, with less damage to his self-esteem. He was less in conflict this time than the time before. I think this is a concept we can all appreciate if we look back at our own lives. I know this particular situation because I was the man involved!

All these principles affect whether or not we'll go into conflict over a given situation. They're all variable, and all depend on circumstances and how life is generally treating us on that particular day, but they all affect us strongly.

4

When the Fan Belt Breaks
or
Situational Sources
of Conflict

Now would be a good time to look at situations in our environment that become occasions of conflict for us. It's important to remember as we consider these situations that they are not conflicts but problems to be faced. We are the ones who turn them into conflicts. We could say the issue is not the issue, people are the issue.

Nevertheless, there's a real world out there, and each of us has a personal history of interacting with it. Our unique backgrounds make us vulnerable to distress in different ways.

For example, my mother married late in life and I was her only child. She was delighted with motherhood and devoted to guiding me according to her understanding of what was best for me. This was fine while I was young, but by the time I was a teenager, I'd begun to resent her close direction and was eager to assert my independence. All teenagers feel this way, no matter how old their parents are, but our relationship was affected by the fact that she was in her mid-fifties, set in her ways, and determined to keep me in control at a time when all my energies were directed toward freedom. She was often impatient and domineering; I was stubborn and angry. I spent a good part of my teenage years in conflict because of these factors.

This part of my past still affects me today whenever I work with women between fifty and sixty. Because of my earlier problems with my mother, I am over-sensitive and defensive with women this age, turning problems between us into conflicts. The problem is mine, not theirs, but it does influence my life and relationships.

In *Games People Play*, Eric Berne says, "Every game begins with a hook." Hooks are the unique and idiosyncratic susceptibilities each of us lives with. They come from our past and make us "conflict prone" in our own personal ways. Not all the hooks we'll discuss will apply to everyone, but understanding conflict is made much easier when we understand our vulnerabilities.

Sigmund Freud observed that we face three basic kinds of frustration in life: the physical world, our own limitations, and other people. Almost any frustration I can think of falls into one of these categories.

The Physical World

The physical world is capable of frustrating anybody, if you think about it. By *physical world*, I mean everything that's not human: nature, machines, animals, potholes, and institutions (which are technically human but behave as inhuman entities much of the time). Most of the physical world appears to operate under some strange mechanical laws that humans were not designed to understand or appreciate.

Almost every day, we run head-on into some of these laws. Flat tires, leaking roofs, burned meals, storms, power failures, airline delays, termite damage, and computer failures are just some examples of the physical world frustrations we must cope with.

Only if you're a prisoner who escapes when the walls fall down will you see an earthquake as a blessing. In fact, this happened during World War I, in Belgium. The walls of a mental institution fell in during a bombing raid, and the patients walked off into the countryside, where they joined the rest of the population and were never found. You may have seen the film *The King of Hearts*. It was based on this incident where good came out of bad. However, generally when the physical world goes wrong, we tend to experience frustration.

A good part of the time, the physical world is beautiful, as is a sunset, an ocean wave, or a devoted pet. Other times, it's at least manageable, as with a broken VCR, an argument about a credit-card error, or directions written in Japanese. But when the physical world goes awry, it can be frustrating and frightening.

On the first night of Basic Mountaineering Training, the Sierra Club shows *The Mountains Don't Care*, a film meant to warn people to be careful while mountain climbing. It shows every conceivable kind of accident that could occur as a result of flash floods, snow white-outs, loose rocks, temperature changes, storms, falling trees, and so on. It's message is, "There's a lot out there in nature that will do people damage without shedding a tear."

The important thing to realize is that even major frustrations with the physical world don't have to become occasions for going into conflict. There are many handicapped people in the world who live with constant physical frustration but never let it dominate them or cause them to go into conflict. They do what they have to do to survive and overcome their physical limitations the best they can, shaming those of us who kick our cars and hurt our toes on a flat tire. It's all in how you handle it.

However, having had a number of personal experiences with physical frustrations can predispose people to "catastrophize" this type of problem and make them feel their self-esteem is in danger. A father who has never once successfully put together a child's toy will look at the words *some assembly required* with considerably more stress than an engineer would. An airline stewardess who has survived a crash will be much more concerned about the age of the aircraft she's on than a newcomer who has been on the job six months.

Personal Limitations

None of us is perfect, and we all have to live with our own personal limitations. My oldest son dreamed of playing major-college football from his first day of high school. He trained well and played hard. He was rewarded with varsity honors, was captain of his high school team, was voted most valuable player at several games, and received regional all-star recognition. Then the time came for college scholarships. My son was six feet tall, and . . . when fattened up . . . weighed no more than 225 pounds. This sounds big, but it didn't impress the UCLA coach. The coach chose a heavier lineman from a nearby high school, even though my son had moved this player handily in past games. He explained to my son, "I can teach that player to block. I can't make you any heavier. You just aren't big enough to play on a major college line."

My son's dreams came crashing down. No other college offered him a scholarship. He could very well have gone into depression, but he didn't. He treated his limitations as a problem to be faced, played football at a local junior college, then finished his last two years on the team of a small university.

We all have limitations and handicaps. Our bodies change on us when we're not looking. A man may have once won a trophy for finishing a ten-mile race, but suddenly discovers he can't run one mile without pain. But this need not be experienced as a conflict unless the man "catastrophizes" the situation. The Special Olympics for the handicapped is an example of people who know how to keep problems from becoming conflicts.

Hospital interns and residents often complain they are being asked to work hours that bus drivers would not be allowed to work. The doctors point out that they are being asked to deal with matters of life and death when they are so tired they are incapable of making rational decisions. Their very human personal limitations are being stretched past the point of frustration, into conflict for them — and danger for their patients. But some doctors excuse themselves, practice relaxation exercises, then return to their duties. They refuse to let problems become conflicts.

The computer is a dramatic testimony to the type of human limitations with which we must live. Computers can calculate much more quickly and accurately than we can. They store information and retrieve it with an agility that far outdistances humans, who are constantly plagued with memory loss and perceptual distortion. Computers, like telephones, compensate for the fact that we cannot be in two places at once, and that information gets distorted by our own limitations. Anyone who has ever played the childhood game of Gossip knows the truth of this statement.

The writer of the Book of Psalms speaks of God knowing who we are, ". . . he remembers that we are dust. As for man, his days are like grass; he flourishes like a flower of the field; for the wind passes over it, and it is gone, and its place knows it no more" (Psalms 103:14, 16). It's very difficult for us to accept the fact that we are only human.

Shakespeare speaks of the world as a stage and humans as mere players who act out different roles during their lives. Realizing we are creatures who ultimately will die has led philosophers to assert that life's dominant emotion is anxiety, the result of frustration we experience from our personal limitations. But, this anxiety over our limitations does not necessarily mean we will go into conflict and engage in drastic measures to restore our endangered self-esteem.

Other People

The final source of frustration mentioned by Freud is other people. There is no doubt in my mind that other people are the major source of frustrations that provoke conflict in us. We are dependent on others from birth to grave. As we noted earlier, self-esteem is always social; other people function as mirrors for us. We think we are who we see ourselves to be, when we judge what others think of us. Our identity (the roles we play) and our status (the reputation we have) are both dependent on other people. We cannot escape the threat that comes from disapproval and resistance.

Garrison Keillor, on one of his "Prairie Home Companion" radio broadcasts, told about David's desire to invite a woman he had met on vacation to Lake Wobegon for Thanksgiving. As he debated with himself whether this was wise or not, he thought of the relatives who would be at Thanksgiving dinner. He wished he could change them, but he feared he could not. He was afraid he would lose any relationship he had with his new lady friend if she were exposed to his relatives. His Uncle Joe would no doubt retell his three classic dirty jokes, before young and old alike, soon after they sat down to eat. This would be embarrassing. His Auny Mary would no doubt go into a long speech about food poisoning and ask many questions about where the food came from and how it was prepared. His friend would question Aunt Mary's sanity. He decided not to invite her. This is the kind of frustration that can come from other people.

Often the frustration of dealing with others is more serious than that. Take the case of a church elder whose mother died after a long illness. He decided to give flower vases for the church altar in her honor. He found some he liked and offered the money for the purchase at a meeting of the church board. He wanted to have the vases on the altar by the time of his mother's birthday some three weeks hence. The board accepted his offering with appreciation, but the discussion took a turn that frustrated him. Some other elders questioned whether they could not get better vases for the same price by looking around at other suppliers. A motion passed to establish a committee to report back to the board a month later — well after his mother's birthday. The elder got red in the face and became furious. Tears flooded his eyes, he went into conflict and left the meeting, saying, "You never pay any attention to my ideas or my wishes. I'm leaving!"

Although the delay in purchasing the vases was not the conflict and the elder could have reacted more calmly to the situation, the meeting was the *occasion* for him to go into conflict. This problem illustrates the way people can frustrate us by differing on the ways, or the means, of achieving goals.

The other board members did not disagree with the elder on the ends or the means. They were all agreed that vases should be purchased. Nor did they disagree with him on the means — he was donating the money, and they accepted it with appreciation. They differed with him on the way to go about the purchase. He had looked in only one catalog. He wanted to buy certain vases, and he wanted to order them immediately. They differed with him on the process to be followed, and this frustrated him and threw him into conflict.

People can also frustrate us by violating the social contract — the tacit agreements that make it possible for us to live together in safety and security. We depend on others to keep up their part of the bargain, and when they do not live up to our expectations, it frustrates us.

I had an experience that demonstrates this point. The fan belt broke on an antique car I was restoring. I saw the temperature was rising, and I smelled steam. Stopping at the first repair shop I passed, I asked the mechanic to replace my fan belt. He refused, saying he was busy, though he was doing nothing! I pointed this out to him. He replied that the job was too difficult. "A fan belt is a fan belt. What do you mean, it's too difficult?" I asked. He shrugged his shoulders and walked away. He just didn't want to work on my antique car. I nursed the car along for several more blocks to a service station that replaced the belt with dispatch.

However, I didn't lose my bitterness about the first man's refusal to help me. I passed his shop often, hoping I would see it closed and boarded shut. My pride was hurt. He didn't do what a repairman was supposed to do, and I wanted him to fail so my self-esteem would be restored.

Yet another way people can frustrate us is by resisting our desires. This can vary from something as trivial as friends not replying to a party invitation, to a maid's failure to clean the stairs as instructed, to a spouse's avoidance of sexual relations. Our pride gets hurt. Our sense of power can be gravely threatened by these frustrations. They can become occasions for going into conflict to protect our reputation and our identity.

The physical world, our personal limitations, and other people provide the occasions to which we may react by going into conflict. While any of these frustrations could be the occasion for us to undertake drastic action to maintain our self-esteem, those situations with which we have had the most experience are likely to cause us the most trouble. Our personal histories will make us more vulnerable to conflict over certain situations.

I mentioned Eric Berne's statement that "Every game begins with a hook." We should remember how Berne defines a game. Games are serious business to Berne, he is not referring to harmless party games that are played for pleasure. All games are harmful, not harmless. They prevent relationships from progressing toward intimacy. Games are played by people in conflict who are not trying to relate, but who are trying to protect and defend themselves. Neither games nor conflicts are constructive. They are sad, tragic efforts of people trying to defend themselves against psychological death.

5

Mowing the Half-Acre Lawn
or
Ways to Reduce Conflict

Anyone who's ever been in the army has heard the saying — "There's the right way, the wrong way, and the army way." As far as the army goes, it's true. I can remember eating breakfast at 5:00 A.M. so we could be on the artillery firing range by 6:00 A.M. for firing practice that was scheduled to begin at 9:00 A.M. It made no sense to me to be three hours early and have to stand around idle, but that's the way the battalion commander planned it, and that's the way it was done. On this and many other occasions I learned to "hurry up and wait."

Eventually I decided that the army way wasn't a matter of being right or wrong — it was just different. Someone higher up saw some form of logic to the army way, so we learned to shrug it off and say, "There's the right way, the wrong way, and the army way." It was something beyond our understanding, but we couldn't really say it was *wrong*.

To some, it even began to make sense. A friend of mine who was a supply officer told me, "It took me six months to learn the system, but after that time it began to make sense to me. I understand it now."

It's the same with reducing conflict. There are three basic ways to reduce conflict, none of which is right or wrong. They're just different. All of them make sense, depending on your point of view, and all of them will reduce a person's conflict, even though each is based on a different premise.

When people in conflict act strangely, they have their own reasons, just as my battalion commander had a reason for getting us to the firing range three hours early. All human behavior is based on some premise or rationale — not necessarily one that's understandable — and the rationale will differ from person to person. As we consider the three ways to reduce conflict, we'll look at what people do and why they do it, since each of these techniques has its own assumptions about what's going on and what should be done to remedy the situation. People attempt to reduce conflict in one of these three ways: the *combat* way, the *conventional* way, and the *Christian* way. The chart on these conflict reducers summarizes the assumptions that lie behind each way. (*See* Conflict Chart.)

Conflict Chart

Assumptions	Combat Way	Conventional Way	Christian Way
What's Happening	Rejection	Misunder-standing	Forgetfulness Ignorance
What Should Be Done	Defense	Justice	Acceptance

The Combat Way

People reacting to conflict with combat assumptions assume that their feelings of low self-esteem are the result of others' intentional rejection of them. Such people assume that people only live for themselves and there is no social contract demanding that people have goodwill toward one another or that people treat one another fairly. According to the combat premise, people are self-centered individuals who are quite willing to discount and use one another. If by some chance some people do obey a social contract, the combat individual thinks they are doing so only because it's in their own best interest. Combat assumptions say that people will always take care of themselves first, even if they have to reject or step on the shoulders of others to do so. If being evil means being selfish, combat assumptions believe people are naturally evil.

People working with these assumptions will use self-defense to restore their self-esteem, since they think no one else in the world would be willing to come to their aid, and the insult was intentional, deserving harsh retaliation. They'll see no sense at all in reasoning with someone who's hurt them; the only person one can trust is oneself. The combat way sees people as dangerous, and when people like this are in conflict, the only way they can reduce it is to take things into their own hands. To them, life is a battle only they can win for themselves. Defense is the name of the game. In fact, the best defense is a good offense, as the old saying goes.

The Conventional Way

The conventional way is recommended by many experts in the field of conflict management. It is based on the premise that justice is what makes society function on a daily basis. Justice is effective because people support the social contract that expects them to treat one another with respect and fairness. This means we can trust one another, assume we'll get value received for money paid, and be socially rewarded for doing unto others as we would have them do unto us.

People working with these assumptions will still go into conflict when their self-esteem is damaged, but they'll assume it was either a misunderstanding or a problem that can be resolved through reason and discussion. Since they see people as naturally good, not evil, they assume that others will make the necessary corrections once they understand this point of view. If they don't, well, that's what the courts are for, and people can always get justice through them if all else fails.

Conventional people are more likely to allow others to help them regain their self-respect. They realize that third parties — a mutual friend or an unbiased mediator — can be helpful in conflicts because they can see both sides without emotional involvement. They don't feel they have to take matters into their own hands because they trust others to respect justice as much as they do. They trust the social process to restore their self-esteem. Justice will win because people are made that way and have good intentions.

The Christian Way

The Christian way is based on a third set of assumptions, not on trust or suspicion. Christian logic begins with the assumption that people sometimes forget where their real security lies. Instead of trying to restore their self-esteem through reasoning or defending themselves, Christians focus their attention on God's love for them as revealed in Jesus Christ. Once they believe in this love — or remember it, if they've forgotten it — their self-esteem is restored and they're no longer in conflict. Acceptance of the truth of God's love reduces the Christian's conflict. How can your self-esteem be in danger when God Himself has declared His love for you so clearly? Remembering or discovering this truth will always reduce distress.

The Lawn

As an illustration of these three ways to reduce conflict, let me tell you about my lawn. I once lived in a house with a backyard that covered nearly half an acre. One Saturday afternoon the lawn needed mowing, so I asked my sons to help me with it. They did for a short while. Then, they remembered a television program they wanted to watch. After that, several of their friends came over; then their uncle dropped by to spend some time with them. It soon became obvious that my help was otherwise occupied.

We had plans to go to a ball game that afternoon and then have a picnic. As the afternoon wore on and it came close to the time to leave for the game, I was still out there, cutting away grimly by myself. The grass was high, the mower was dull, and I didn't think I'd be done in time. From inside the house came the sounds of happy laughter and conversation.

No one was even thinking about me. No one cared that I might miss the ball game. All they cared about was having fun. Let good old Dad take care of himself! To put it mildly, my self-esteem was threatened. I was unloved, insecure, and unimportant to my family. I was in conflict.

Sure, it was a little thing to go into conflict over, but it doesn't always take big things to upset us. By now, I was so upset that I didn't care whether the lawn ever got done; I just wanted someone to pay me some attention and fix my self-esteem.

I had three ways to reduce my conflict and restore my feelings of self-worth: combat, conventional, and Christian. Let's see what would have happened if I'd tried each of them.

Combat

Had I decided to use the combat way, I would have assumed my family had chosen to ignore me and intentionally left me out there alone. I would have kicked the lawn mower, turned it off, marched angrily to my car, and driven off to a movie by myself. Because we had only one car, that would have stranded the rest of the family at home. I would have been thinking, *Since they don't love and respect me, I'll show them! Let's see them get to the game without me. I have to take care of myself. Who cares what happens to their day? I should know better than to expect any help or concern from them!*

If there wasn't a movie I wanted to see and I still wanted to use the combat way, I could have stormed into the house and used the direct approach, yelling at my sons to turn off the TV and get to work out back. I could have snarled at my wife and brother-in-law and generally punished everyone by refusing to let them go on the planned outing.

All of these actions would have been based on the assumption that my family had purposely insulted me and didn't care about me in the least. If this were true, it would be up to me to take care of myself, to defend myself against these threats to my self-respect and sense of worth. I would avoid my family, be demanding, force them, punish them — all without discussion, since they were undependable.

Conventional

Had I decided to turn off the mower, go into the house, and call a family conference, I would have been using the conventional way of reducing my conflict. I would assume there was no ill will in their actions and that they still appreciated me. Once I explained my problem to them, they'd see the light and help me finish the job in time for the game, because they would be fair and helpful. My self-esteem would have been quickly repaired by their coming out to help me, and we'd all get to enjoy our outing. There'd be no unilateral action, no yelling, no punishment — reason and logic would win the day and restore my self-esteem.

Christian

If I had chosen the Christian way to restore my self-esteem, I would have had several choices. I might have stopped the mower and bowed my head in prayer, asking God to remind me I was a valuable, precious person to Him, and I had no reason to be afraid or feel threatened. I'd remind myself of the passage, "Cast all your anxieties on him, for he cares for you" (1 Peter 5:7).

Or I could have gone inside and opened my Bible to Luke:

> . . . Therefore, I tell you, do not be anxious about your life, what you shall eat, nor about your body, what you shall put on. For life is more than food, and the body more than clothing. Consider the ravens: they neither sow nor reap, they have neither storehouse nor barn, and yet God feeds them. Of how much more value are you than the birds! And which of you by being anxious can add a cubit to his span of life? If then you are not able to do as small a thing as that, why are you anxious about the rest? Consider the lilies, how they grow; they neither toil nor spin; yet I tell you, even Solomon in all his glory was not arrayed like one of these. But if God so clothes the grass which is alive in the field today and tomorrow is thrown into the oven, how

much more will he clothe you, O men of little faith!

Luke 12:22–28

Once I felt reassured of God's love for me, I might have calmly asked my family for help or gone back to work alone. If I didn't finish the job in time for the game, I would have let it wait for me. In other words, my self-esteem would be high enough for me to deal with the problem without feeling threatened.

For the combat way, the big question is: How can I best protect myself from other people's evil intentions? The motto is: I'm okay, but you're not okay, and I'll fight for my rights. The front of a combat sweatshirt reads: Don't let the scum get you down. The back carries the message: Be prepared.

For the conventional way, the big question is: When can we get together and hear each other's side of the story? The motto is: I'm okay and you're okay, and we can work it out. The front of a conventional sweatshirt would read: Fairness to all. The back would proclaim: Be calm and trust the process.

For the Christian way, the big question is: Why do I keep forgetting who I really am? The motto is: I'm not okay, you're not okay, but that's okay. The Christian sweatshirt reads: Be of good cheer; I have overcome the world, and, remember Calvary.

Do They Work?

Will the combat, conventional, and Christian ways to reduce conflict actually work? Yes! Each of them will effectively reduce the conflict inside people and restore their self-esteem. They take people out of distress, downgrading it to simple stress, and making problem solving possible.

But possibilities are not promises. There's no guarantee that people will successfully solve the problems that put them into conflict in the first place, even though they're now capable of working on it. All these techniques do is remove the conflict for a while and make effective action possible.

The best example of conflict reduction that did not result in the successful solution of a problem is that of Jesus in the garden of Gethsemane. Jesus experienced a great deal of distress in the garden. The Bible states that He prayed, "Father, if thou art willing, remove this cup from me . . . not my will, but thine, be done." An angel from heaven appeared to Him and strengthened Him. In great anguish He prayed even more fervently; His sweat was like drops of blood, falling to the ground. (*See* Luke 22:42–44 KJV.)

Jesus was not just experiencing stress; He was in distress. He would have preferred to have returned to Nazareth and live a normal lifespan, not die on a cross in early manhood. Then an angel came and strengthened Him, reducing His conflict and restoring His self-esteem. "Nevertheless not my will, but thine, be done," He declared, getting up and going forth to face His accusers.

Jesus could have solved His problem by calling down angels to devastate His persecutors, by using the power that was His to use, but He didn't. He told His disciples to put away their swords, restored the ear of the high priest's slave, and allowed Himself to be arrested.

It is clear that while confrontation with His accusers was stressful, it was not distressful. Jesus was no longer in conflict. He was prepared to die rather than deny that He was the Son of God, the long-hoped-for Messiah.

By worldly standards, Jesus didn't solve His problem: He died. On the other hand, His death was God's will, and no one can say He failed.

Conflict resolution is no guarantee that our problems will be solved, but conflict reduction through the combat, conventional, or Christian way is a guarantee that people will no longer be in distress. At least for a time, self-esteem will be restored enough so that problem solving becomes a possibility, even if it is not a certain probability.

Part II
The Combat Way

6

Sending the Bags to Hong Kong
or
The Combat Way

People attempting to reduce their conflict through use of the combat approach see their problems from a unique perspective. They assume, first of all, that whatever they feel to be true is true. As I have indicated before, when they feel rejected, in their minds they have been rejected. When they feel discounted, attacked, belittled, and vilified, they believe their feelings are based on objective truth. The combat approach assumes that people have intentionally gone out of their way to attack us and cannot be counted on to understand our distress.

Remember, people in conflict may not act rationally. The most wonderful, kind, and loving people you know may attempt to reduce their conflict using combat techniques and see things in a totally unreasonable way, turning into someone you don't even know anymore. The fact that they haven't been rejected, and you can see that clearly, is not at all important. What matters is how the person in conflict sees things. People who use the combat way to reduce their conflict are not bad or unpleasant people in their normal lives, nor are they crazy when in conflict. Unpleasant perhaps; certainly irrational; but not crazy.

Combat Techniques

People who use combat to reduce their conflict typically react in one of three ways: They compete, accommodate, or avoid. The technique they choose at any given time is usually based on their past experience, but the choice is rarely thought out. No one in conflict stops and thinks, *Well, I think I'll try avoidance this time.* The choice is made impulsively, but the underlying assumption is always that whichever technique is used, people are all alone and must defend themselves.

When we're rational, we consider both the problem and the person related to it, in other words. In the case of our young mother hearing bad news about her son from the neighbor, a person not in conflict would consider both the source and the report and react appropriately to both.

But a person in conflict will emphasize either the issue or the other person involved. Our young mother felt her status as a mother was in danger and ignored the issue to attack the other mother. Once she got rolling, Tommy's name and behavior were never mentioned again; she ignored the issue to concentrate on her *enemy*. She could have said, "Well, you're not such a good mother yourself. Look at your children. My Tommy has never done what your Mary did!" She could just as well have gone the other way and put her effort into regaining the other mother's respect by saying, "Tell me everything you know. I respect your opinion, and I'll punish Tommy when he comes home. I hope you won't think less of me for Tommy's behavior." Finally, she could have hung up the phone and refused to deal with the problem.

One way we might conceive of these alternative concerns for persons and problems has been proposed by Jane Mouton and Robert Blake in their book *The Managerial Grid.*

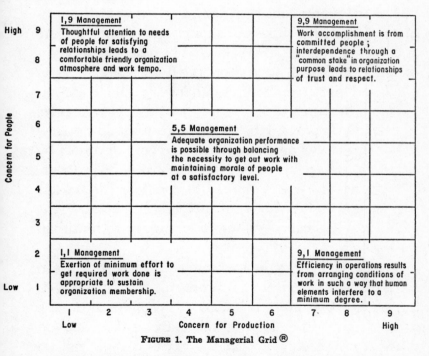

FIGURE 1. The Managerial Grid ®

Reprinted with permission from R.R. Blake and J.S. Mouton. *The Managerial Grid* (Houston, Texas: Gulf Publishing Company, 1964, 1969), p. 10.

My analysis of these issues is not exactly like Blake and Mouton's, but the Grid diagram shows how concerns for persons and for problems might be put in juxtaposition to one another.

The Grid diagram indicates how competition, accommodation, and avoidance relate to one another. The two dimensions of the Grid refer to the degree to which people put emphasis on maintaining the goodwill of others or on being victorious over them.

People who must dominate in order to feel good about themselves will compete when they are in conflict. Our young soldier in the jungle was in the ultimate competitive situation: submit and die or compete and live. He didn't care at all what his enemies thought of him! Dr. Kelno, who cooperated with the Nazis in *QB VII*, didn't care about dominance at all. He accommodated because Nazi approval, which kept him alive, was vitally important to him. Those who do not feel they can succeed or maintain the support of others by asserting their point of view tend to avoid the problem. The church elder who wanted to donate the vases left the meeting when he went into conflict because the goodwill of his peers was more important to him than the vases.

Avoidance falls at the extreme ends of both concern for persons and concern for problems. It reflects a feeling of isolation and an inability to dominate on the issue. Competition falls at the extreme low end on concern for persons and at the extreme high end on concern for winning. It reflects the feeling that one is alone but can win the point through aggressiveness. Accommodation falls at the low end of concern for the problem and at the extreme end of concern for the persons with whom one is relating. Here persons feel they cannot influence the decision to win the point and that their only way to salvage some good feelings of friendship is to give in.

In his book *Reaching Out*, D. W. Johnson compares people who use avoidance to turtles who pull into their shells during times of danger. Those who compete are like sharks who force their way on others without any regard for their survival or feelings. Accommodators are teddy bears who will do anything to avoid the ill will of others. Their prime concern is to smooth things out so people will think well of them.

Further, these three reactions could also be looked at in win/lose terms. If I engage in all-out combat with you, one of us will win and the other will lose. If I accommodate, you will win and I'll lose. If I try avoidance, we'll both lose.

Regardless of the type of reaction, in reality nobody wins. If one of us wins by defeating the other, the loser is humiliated and devastated, and the relationship is destroyed. If you win because I give in and accommodate, I still won't be convinced you're right, and the problem isn't solved. If I choose avoidance, neither of us wins and the problem still exists.

People who choose the combat way to reduce their conflict rarely use just one of these techniques. They'll choose the one that promises the best results or use all three in sequence. First they'll try to stick to their opinion and dominate. If that doesn't work, they'll try accommodation or finally retreat from the scene to maintain the relationship. The important thing is that all three of these reactions are combative in nature. Even a soldier who retreats in battle is still a soldier, not a diplomat.

Another important point to remember is that none of these techniques solves problems. Their only goal is the reduction of inner conflict. Many times it may appear as if the problem has been solved through competition, accommodation, or avoidance, but it only looks that way. The person will feel better, but the problem still exists and will cause further conflict the next time it comes up. However, the combat way is still useful because it does reduce conflict and return rationality to the scene, and only then can progress be made toward solving the problem itself.

Competition

The word *competition* doesn't do justice to the desperation people who use this technique feel; it's too polite a word. Confrontation might express it better, since it denotes a struggle, because the fact is, in competition that's designed to increase a person's self-esteem, we're talking about a major battle where one side is out to annihilate the other!

I was reminded of this the time I visited Universal Studios and saw their animated display of King Kong. Kong is the epitome of confrontation, symbolizing a fight to the finish. He overwhelms his opposition and asserts his will over anyone standing in his way. Anyone in the way of people's use of competition to repair their damaged self-esteem is facing a force as wild, unreasoning, and untamable as King Kong. But don't forget, Kong was a perfectly acceptable and lovable animal before he went into conflict.

People in conflict who react competitively see the other person as a mortal enemy who cannot be allowed to win. If the enemy wins, the conflicted person's self-esteem will die. In his book *Games People Play*, Eric Berne described a game called Now I've Got You, You SOB. In this game, people manipulate the situation through force and connivance until the opponent is figuratively lying helpless on his or her back in surrender. This is a good illustration of the intent behind competitive combat reactions.

In conflict terms, a person's self-esteem is not restored until the opponent surrenders everything. This helps people in conflict regain self-esteem but usually results in the victim going into conflict as a result of humiliation. It's a case of "I win/you lose" — all the way to the bitter end. The result, of course, is that the problem isn't solved and isn't likely to be solved until the victim comes out of conflict. Two people could go on like this for years! As horrible as that would be in a personal relationship, think what it could do to a business.

Nevertheless, people who make combat assumptions when they go into conflict are likely to try competition before accommodation or avoidance. Everyone likes to win, and this is the only combat technique where someone seems to win. We in the West seem particularly attached to this technique because it tells people we are independent, self-confident people. We are brought up to protect our rights and assert ourselves, so it seems natural to us to do this when we go into conflict.

Who's Afraid of Virginia Wolf?

For example, a married couple arguing over a specific expense may find the discussion escalating until one or both are in conflict. Then past disagreements about money will be mentioned, old hurts resurrected, and problems not even related to the original question tossed in for effect. As the evening goes on, the only way the argument will ever come to an end is if one person admits he or she was totally wrong on *all* counts, and that's not likely to happen. Bringing old hurts into a disagreement like this is called "gunnysacking," a particularly common but unproductive trick we all use from time to time.

The difficulty of total surrender was graphically brought out in the movie *Who's Afraid of Virginia Wolf?* The husband (Richard Burton) was a college professor who never got promoted. His wife (Elizabeth Taylor) couldn't get pregnant. Yet they started every dinner with the following exchange:

"Did you get a promotion today?"

"Did you get pregnant yet?"

Every night, things would go from bad to worse until both were in conflict and yelling. Neither ever won, and they grew farther and farther apart each evening.

This type of stalemate happens when two people go into conflict at the same time and both take a competitive stance. Neither party ever has his or her self-esteem restored, the problem is never discussed rationally, and the situation becomes permanently stalemated.

Rebuilding the Y's

A community discussion over the building of a new YMCA/YWCA building in Pasadena, California, almost turned into such a stalemate. There were four sides to the controversy. Both organizations wanted to construct a new building on ground adjacent to the present YWCA. Their plans called for the destruction of a wing of the YWCA that had been built after the main building was completed in the 1920s.

This building plan was opposed by the Pasadena Heritage Association, which wanted the buildings preserved because they were the work of an early twentieth-century female architect. A group of athletic-club owners opposed the new building because they saw it as unfair competition paid for by public funds. Those who lived at the YMCA or YWCA would lose their low-rent housing, which was one of their main services, so they were opposed to the new building, too.

The local newspaper was wise enough to see a major confrontation brewing, and it called for all those involved to calm down and deal with the issues as problems to be solved rather than victories to be won. Had the controversy escalated, I have no doubt that people on every side would have gone into conflict, but fortunately that didn't happen and an agreement was reached before they came to a stalemate.

Aggression Versus Assertion

Competition is sometimes obscured by logic. Points of view become tied to logical rationales that seem airtight to those espousing them. As the frustration of disagreement mounts, the imposition of logic becomes more heavy-handed, until people are in conflict and what seemed a reasonable discussion has turned into outright aggression.

One of the first signs that people are in conflict is when they cease to assert their opinions and turn aggressive. At this point you can be sure they feel their self-esteem is in danger and the need to destroy their opponents is now more important than the original disagreement. Their assertion has turned into aggression.

In our book *Speak Up!* Randy Sanders and I discussed the differences between assertion and aggression. Assertive people express their rights and opinions while respecting and allowing others to express their own rights and opinions. Aggressive people express their rights and opinions at others' expense. At its most extreme, competition as a conflict reaction is aggression, not assertion.

The Use of Power in Aggression

Power can often camouflage aggressive competitiveness. The opinions of those with power always have more effect than those of the powerless. When a powerful person's opinions are resisted, however, the person will sometimes use power in place of logic. People who say, "Do it because I say so!" may be in conflict and using their power as a way to restore their endangered self-esteem.

Take the case of Donald, a young seminary graduate in his first full-time ministry. He was employed as an associate of Wayne, a pastor with thirty-five years experience who had had only one other assistant during his ministry. At the very beginning of their relationship, Wayne called Donald into his office and said, "I would think it best that you consider me the boss. Anytime you have any plans or ideas, come to me, and we'll discuss them. I'll decide whether you should do something or not. Okay?"

Donald thought nothing of this arrangement, since this was his first assignment and Wayne had so much experience. One day Donald approached Wayne about working out at the local YMCA before coming to work in the morning. He would arrive at the church at 8:15 instead of 8:00. Wayne replied, "Go ahead. That's okay. I wish I could join you, but these bones are getting too old for such exercise."

So Donald bought a membership at the YMCA and proceeded to work out each morning before coming to the church. He kept his agreement and arrived by 8:15 every day.

Two weeks later, Wayne called Donald into his office and stated, "Donald, I think it would be best if you didn't work out anymore."

"Why, Wayne? What's the problem?"

"You've been late, and I don't think that's fair to the church," Donald replied.

"But that's not fair. I was only late one day. Be reasonable. I promise I won't be late anymore."

"I think you should quit. Don't go anymore."

"Well, suppose I go from five to six, after office hours are over?"

"Donald, you don't have office hours. A minister is on call twenty-four hours a day."

A few exchanges later, Wayne shouted, "Donald, you are not going to work out at all! Do you understand? I'm the boss, and I'm telling you what to do!"

"Well, I guess we'll just have to let the board decide, won't we?" Donald shot back as he left the office.

At the next board meeting, Donald explained the situation. When the board asked to hear Wayne's side, he simply replied, "I don't think it's the best use of Donald's time." To Donald's surprise, the board agreed with Wayne and ordered Donald to stop his workouts.

Over the next six months, Donald continued to bring Wayne his plans and get his approval before going ahead. On three occasions, Wayne approved an idea with the stipulation that they go before the board and let them know what was being planned. Each time,

Wayne would tell the board, "I don't think it's a good idea."

After this happened three times, Donald went to the chair of the board and explained his problem with Wayne. The chair replied, "Donald, I know what you're going through. He did the same thing to the other youth minister. We can't afford to lose Wayne, but I'll be praying for you."

The next time Donald had a project he wanted to undertake, he didn't tell Wayne anything about it. He presented it to the board, which passed it unanimously before Wayne even had a chance to speak against it.

The next morning Wayne called Donald into his office. "Donald, why didn't you come to me before you went to the board?"

"Because every time I come to you, you tell me one thing and then do something else when we go to the board. You've stabbed me in the back too many times, Wayne. I can't trust you."

"But I'm the boss!" Wayne shouted.

"Not when you do things like this. From now on I'm going to act as if I can't trust you. I won't come to you. I can't afford to. It's too frustrating and distressing for me." Donald turned on his heel and walked out of the office.

Wayne sat at his desk, dumbfounded. He couldn't believe what he'd just heard from his assistant. He thought back on his thirty-five years of ministry. No one had ever talked to him like that before!

This form of competitive aggression involves an imperialistic assertion of rights over others. Once these people win, they become paternalistic and indulgent, but they are still using their power to get their way and reduce their own distress.

Aggression and Relationships

Our willingness to be aggressive when we are competing is sometimes a function of the closeness of the relationship with our *enemy*. Although it's easier for my self-esteem to be threatened by someone I'm dependent on, I'm more likely to use aggression in more casual relationships. Our relationships with others exist on a scale of dependency running from one-time contacts to our relationships with our spouses.

- One-time contacts: A person in a passing car or in line in a supermarket.
- Commercial contacts: A car salesman, travel agent, or clerk in a store.
- Acquaintances: A colleague at work, a fellow club member.
- Friends: A longtime associate, a friendly neighbor.
- Lovers: A person in a romantic encounter.
- Intimates: A person I share deeply with, male or female.

When my self-esteem is threatened and I go into conflict, I'm more likely to be aggressive with casual acquaintances or one-time contacts than those with whom I am more deeply involved. I have been known at times to shout at fellow drivers in frustration. I usually avoid looking at these people because I'm immediately embarrassed by my actions and am always afraid I might recognize them if I did look!

On one occasion I parked in an area reserved for doctors at a clinic. The attendant didn't care that there were no other available patient spaces and the doctors' area was nearly empty. He told me to move and suggested I was either blind or stupid. I immediately went into conflict, said something less than polite to him, and drove off in a huff, knowing I'd never see him again.

We tend to avoid aggressive responses with those we are dependent on, although they have the power to hurt us the most and throw us into conflict faster than casual contacts. Over the years, my wife and I have learned to argue without being aggressive or needing to win. We're both confident that our self-esteem is not in danger from each other, no matter how upset we may become, and even our children came to realize that our occasionally loud problem solving wasn't a threat to their family life.

Revenge

If the battle is lost, those who use combat techniques invariably begin to think along the lines that revenge is sweet — don't get mad, get even. They've gone into combat to regain their self-esteem and lost, so their conflict still exists and they've lost even more self-esteem.

People in this situation need some form of satisfaction to restore their self-image. They want *retribution:* an eye for an eye, a tooth for a tooth. If they can't have that, they want public justification or financial compensation. They want to settle the score. Only when things have been made even will they feel good again.

Punishment is another form of revenge. Mothers Against Drunk Driving supports punishment. Although nothing will bring back those killed by drunk drivers, punishment of the offenders does help the self-esteem of the victims' survivors and may make others less likely to drive while drunk.

Retaliation is yet another aggressive response to a loss. Israel's foreign policy is based on two words: *Never again.* This is a forewarning that aggression will be met by aggression. It's a strong statement that leaves no doubt about the nation's intentions or its self-image.

Retaliation need not be this direct. Passive aggression refers to those who are not powerful enough to react overtly to hostility. They sabotage, refuse to cooperate, go underground, all of which is still retaliation.

A final form of revenge is *intimidation*, where threats are the primary weapon. Gorillas who beat their chests to scare away enemies are using intimidation, as is a street gang yelling threats to another gang from a distance. Although all revenge is primitive, intimidation is the most sophisticated type of revenge.

No one thinks revenge is socially acceptable, but most of us think about it now and then. A friend of mine was standing in line at an airport, listening to the person ahead of him berate a clerk who was checking him in. When his turn came, my friend said to the clerk, "I admire the way you handled that man who was so hostile and rude to you. You didn't get mad or talk ugly to him. How do you handle such things?"

The clerk smiled and replied, "Well, he's going to San Francisco, but I sent his bags to Hong Kong!" Her self-esteem was just fine, thank you!

7

Guerrilla Warfare and Teddy Bears

or

Accommodation

Competition is the first of three possible combat techniques for reducing conflict; accommodation is the second. Webster defines *accommodation* as, "to bring into agreement or concord: reconcile."

If you're talking about problem solving, this is a good definition. When we're not in conflict, we all use accommodation to resolve disagreements, especially when we feel our relationship with the other person is more important than the issue at hand.

For example, I'm intrigued by those invitations that come in the mail asking me to visit a nearby vacation spot and receive a gift in return for listening to the pitch and taking a tour. I once tried to convince my wife to go with me to a resort that guaranteed we'd receive a savings bond, grandfather clock, free trip to Mexico, or BMW automobile. I couldn't see how we could possibly lose by taking the trip, and we might win something valuable in return for our time.

My wife saw it differently. "Absolutely not! I'm not going to waste my Saturday afternoon on such a wild-goose chase. There has to be a catch," she proclaimed. "When are you going to stop being taken in by such come-ons? You'd think a person with as much education as you have would see through these things!"

Undaunted, I decided to wait a day and bring up the matter again. When I looked for the invitation the following day, I found it in the wastebasket, where my wife had tossed it. As I started to retrieve it, I thought about her previous response. She had been dead serious the day before, and my bringing it up again would only succeed in making her angry, so I decided to leave the invitation in the wastebasket and drop the issue.

This is an example of problem solving through accommodation, as Webster defines it. Avoiding a fight over the issue and not endangering an important relationship was more important to me than the grandfather clock, and I gave in. Once I had accommodated, the matter was over and done with, and I had no regrets about my action, no hard feelings, and no desire for revenge. I'd never gone into conflict over the issue, so my self-esteem was intact. In problem-solving situations where no one is in conflict, accommodation is a fair and useful technique for resolving differences.

Accommodation in Conflict

Accommodation has an entirely different meaning when conflict is involved, however. Historically, only losers accommodate. They surrender and strike the best bargain they can to maintain their self-esteem. Argentina gave in to England on the Falkland Island dispute when it became obvious that England was willing and able to defend her claim to the islands. There was no chance that Argentina could win an all-out war with England, so to avoid utter defeat, they accommodated. Likewise, since the Seven Day War of 1967, Israel has controlled the West Bank in Palestine. On the surface, the Palestinians surrendered to ensure their survival.

Both of these examples illustrate an important fact of conflict accommodation: It's always an act of survival, but it should never be looked on as an act of agreement. Argentina still believes the Falklands belong to Argentina, not England. The Palestinians on the West Bank live under the Israelis unwillingly, with extreme resistance. In a time of conflict, surrender is almost always only skin-deep.

This is also true on an individual level, where one person gives in to another in defeat. Any agreement the two may work out will be very fragile and not necessarily satisfactory to both parties. First of all, it will be an agreement imposed by the winners. Winners don't need to compromise or take the losers' concerns into consideration, and most don't, with the result that sabotage, revenge, and guerrilla warfare are to be expected when someone has reduced his conflict through accommodation.

I'm reminded of this truth when I think of a particularly offensive but perversely humorous postcard I often saw as I was growing up in Alabama. It showed a uniformed Confederate general standing with feet apart, his sword firmly implanted in the ground, looking out from under his hat with a menacing glare. The line at the bottom of the card read, "Surrender? Never!"

My first memory of this was in the 1940s, some seventy-five years after the South had actually surrendered! But, there were many people in the South still feeling bitterness and humiliation at being defeated by the North, and they identified with this postcard. The flying of the Confederate flag on top of several state capitols is a defiant reminder that even this surrender was only skin-deep. Of course this was not true for everyone in the South, but it was definitely a maxim in my family that you couldn't trust anything said by anyone who came from above the Mason-Dixon line.

One of the episodes on the TV show "The Golden Girls" included a discussion of whether Betty White should date a person from another ethnic background. Rue McClanahan confessed that she had incurred great disapproval from her friends and family for taking a *foreigner* to her senior prom in high school. When asked if her date had been black, Chinese, or some other minority, she replied, "Goodness no! He was Yankee!" I'm thankful that I've outlived this suspicion of Northerners, but the feeling that surrender to the North during the Civil War was more a way to survive than an admission of wrong was very common among the people I grew up with. It illustrates the precarious nature of forced compliance when accommodation has been a combat reaction to conflict.

Most of us have been in this position and understand these feelings quite well. Certain people, such as bosses, policemen, parents, and judges, have power over our lives and assert that power when we disagree with them. We accommodate in these situations because we don't want to be fired, go to jail, or be kicked out of the house, but we don't necessarily agree with the involved people. A teenager who obeys his curfew because he has no other choice may still find ways to come home on time and make life miserable for his parents!

A friend of mine usually finds herself disagreeing with her boss, but one day he went too far and changed her working hours without any discussion or consideration for the other demands on her time. Whereas before she had been able to deal with their disagreements in a reasonable manner, this time she went into conflict, stirred up her colleagues, and explored every possible way to defeat the boss. Finally they knuckled under and agreed to the new working hours. Why? Did they suddenly see the light and agree with him? Of course not! They gave in because they felt it was better to lose the battle than to lose the war (and their jobs). Compliance was a matter of survival, not agreement.

When people in conflict surrender, they do so to prevent their damaged self-esteem from suffering an even worse blow. The self-esteem they gain by surrendering is a fragile one, but it's better than no self-esteem at all.

Unfortunately, the victors in these battles tend to believe the losers are changed people who have seen the light and now agree with them. They want everything to suddenly become friendly, all signs of disagreement to vanish, and goodwill to reign. The victors suddenly become generous to a fault, rebuilding the country they have just destroyed, taking care of the war's victims, making pacts of nonaggression, and so forth. The same thing happens on an individual level when a victorious boss hands out rewards for compliance, or a parent rescinds the harsh punishment imposed on a sullen son who now looks as though he's cooperating.

There's nothing wrong with these peaceful overtures — they may very well lessen the conflict the loser is feeling — but it's foolish to assume that all is forgiven. I became dramatically aware of this while interacting with a former student of mine. She had been a difficult student, and although she completed a respectable dissertation, her clinical work as a psychology intern was replete with problems. She simply could not get along with her colleagues. She manipulated secretaries, forced her opinions on clients, and complained inordinately when she could not change the rules of the clinics in which she worked.

We counseled her long and hard. Finally, she agreed to change and adjusted to the extent that we felt we could pass her. We thought she understood the issue and was committed to being a different kind of psychologist, that we'd all handled the issue reasonably with no one going into conflict, and that all was well between us.

After she graduated, the student dropped out of contact, which was quite different from my relationship with other graduates. I began to suspect that her compliance had not been as wholehearted as I had thought. I wrote a friendly letter to her that was not answered. Finally, I met her face-to-face at a professional meeting and asked if we could meet to work out our relationship.

Instead of meeting me, she sent me a note from which I learned for the first time how hurt and angry she was with me. I had presumed that we had a problem and had worked it out by her giving in to my viewpoint, but the note told me how much she disagreed with us and how angry she still was that she had been forced to comply with our judgments. I hadn't realized how much conflict she was in and that her surrender was not a way of resolving differences, but a way of regaining self-respect and obtaining her degree. I think this is a good illustration of how easy it is to be duped and to confuse problem solving with conflict reaction.

Attempting to reduce conflict and increase self-esteem through surrender is obviously different from solving problems in which the relationship involved is what's important. In conflict, it's often less a matter of relationships and more a matter of forced compliance, where one surrenders in action but not in thought. Bitterness festers and eventually surfaces in acts of sabotage or resistance.

Teddy Bear Accommodation

There are conflicts in which the compliance is real and minds are truly changed. In these cases, you're most probably dealing with the type of person we labeled a *teddy bear*. The problem here is not that the loser surrenders on the surface and never really gives up underneath; here the person *does* give up and surrenders too quickly and easily. Here we see a complete turnaround of opinion that is usually coupled with a desperate dependence on the goodwill of the other party.

The winner in a situation like this should keep in mind that such teddy bears are still reacting in a combative way. The problem hasn't been solved. The person who has surrendered has resolved his internal conflict by changing his mind to please the winner, but he may go into conflict over the same issue again.

Parents quite often fall into this error. All parents prefer peace and quiet at home, but when one tells me that her children are perfect in all respects, I begin to think there's a little teddy-bear conflict accommodation going on inside the child. Children who are *too good* may be good as a drastic reaction to conflict. It's always a good idea to be sure a child isn't giving up his or her integrity in an effort to restore her overdependent self-esteem.

Teddy-bear accommodation makes sense to people because self-esteem is highly dependent on the opinions of others. Most of a young child's identity and status depend on his relationship with his parents. In a way, it makes sense that a child would treat his relationship with his parents as one of great importance, and that the child will give in whenever his opinions threaten that relationship. Employees often feel the same way about their superiors and give in willingly whenever a conflict arises. But, always giving in without a fight should be seen as a denial of what it means to be a valuable human being created by God with self-determination and a mind of one's own. Teddy bears give up too much of themselves and end up destroying the self-esteem they are trying so desperately to protect.

Adults can fall into this type of conflict reaction when they are too needy of another's approval. I once had a husband telephone me in a panic. He said his wife felt that she had married too young and missed out on night life. She wanted to go out at least two nights a week with her girlfriend and be free to spend the night out too. The difficult thing for me to understand was that the husband had agreed to this arrangement for three months before calling me. Even then, he wasn't calling to ask my opinion about this bargain — he'd agreed to that out of his love for her and a need for her approval. Now his wife wanted to move in with her girlfriend and come to see him and their baby one or two nights a week! The husband called me because he didn't know if he could stand up to his wife. He was generally an imposing man with a good deal of status, but his fear of losing his wife had reduced him to jelly. He was too dependent on her and was denying his own self-worth. This is a perfect example of desperate accommodation to conflict when one assumes combat logic.

Those who accommodate to preserve their self-esteem when in conflict are surrendering, but their surrender will be either conditional or unhealthy. They've put themselves in the position of being a loser to protect their lives or a relationship on which they are overdependent. They have not solved the problems behind the conflict and are reacting with a combat technique. This combat technique should not be confused with the healthy accommodation that takes place when no one is in conflict and leads to the resolution of problems. That's a healthy technique, while combat accommodation always has its problems.

8

Learning From Bobby Knight, Flip Wilson, and Cher

or

Avoidance

The third combat technique that people use to reduce their conflict and increase their self-esteem is *avoidance*. Avoidance can be summed up by the phrase, "nobody likes a fight." Again it's important to differentiate between the way we act during unconflicted problem solving and the way we act while in conflict. When we're not in conflict, we tend to see nothing wrong with a good disagreement, and some people do indeed enjoy a fight under these circumstances. But, not when they're in conflict.

Some people seem to be naturally more competitive than others. They enjoy debating points of view because it stimulates them and makes them feel vital and alive. Many of us enjoy watching a good boxing match, a hard-hitting football game, or a violent movie. Others engage in mountain climbing, hang gliding, and other dangerous sports, because they enjoy challenging danger and temporarily defeating death.

There are many couples in this world who seem to spend their entire married lives in combat with each other. They argue every point that comes up, slam doors, and rarely say a good word about each other. This makes people who don't know them well think they hate each other. In fact, many of these couples are deeply devoted, and woe to the outsider who makes a disparaging comment to one of them about the other! They just happen to enjoy their fights, and since neither of them feels his or her self-esteem is threatened by this interaction, neither ever goes into conflict. You might say they're simply loud problem solvers.

But conflict is an entirely different matter. No one *enjoys* being in conflict. The difference between enjoying problem solving and disliking conflict is similar to the difference between riding the ocean's waves and having to fight an undertow. Bodysurfing the incoming waves is fun, even if you get bowled over and drink a little of the ocean now and then. But feeling your legs being pulled out from under you and seeing the shore recede while you frantically swim for your life is frightening. If the lifeguard said that the undertow was dangerous, most of us would stay out of the water to avoid it.

In the same way, some people deal with conflict through avoidance. They don't become competitive and try to win the argument to restore their self-esteem, and they don't surrender and let others dominate them; they avoid it any way they can.

It's possible to avoid conflict before you get enmeshed in it, which is a healthy problem-solving technique. Not going in the water when there's a strong undertow avoids the undertow conflict. Backing off in a disagreement before your self-esteem is threatened is problem solving. When we avoid, to *stay out* of conflict, we're trying our best to keep from crossing the line from stress to distress. We might tell ourselves to calm down, evaluate the true importance of the issues concerned, or walk away from the disagreement. This is avoidance, but since it's done before we're actually in conflict, it remains a valid problem-solving technique.

Conflict Avoidance

Once we're in conflict, we can only restore our self-esteem through competition, accommodation, or avoidance. Those who choose to compete believe they can win through force. They feel equipped to take on all comers, defeat them one by one, and end up on top of the pile. Those who accommodate know they're beaten. They surrender everything to avoid total annihilation and make the best deal they can to restore their self-esteem.

Those who use avoidance are like a retreating army. The battle's lost for the day, so they back off and wait for the situation to change or they turn around and run before they get bowled over. They know when to retreat. Since they haven't actually been annihilated in battle, their self-esteem is restored. This technique is often called a strategic retreat.

A classic example of conflict reduction through avoidance is our military pullout of Vietnam. We tried to compete for years, but a variety of factors made winning impossible. We'd done all we could through competition, but we were a country deep in conflict, internally and externally, and the only way left to salvage our self-esteem was through avoidance. We didn't win the war in Vietman, but no one could say we actually lost it, either. We avoided that by leaving.

Another example of avoidance was when the University of Indiana basketball coach, Bobby Knight, became so infuriated with the officials in a 1987 game that he took his team off the court and refused to finish the game. He was also using avoidance to get out of or reduce his conflict.

There are several different types of conflict avoidance that people use, depending on their personality and the given situation. While they vary in the amount of aggression they display, all are combat reactions used to restore self-esteem, and all illustrate combat mentality in that the person using them is watching out for himself because he trusts no one else. All combat reactions are inherently hostile. Even a retreating army will turn on its enemy if the situation changes and it suddenly feels it can win the battle.

Double-edged Avoidance

Bobby Knight's taking his team off the court and refusing to continue the game is an example of *double-edged* avoidance. It cut two ways. On the one hand,

Knight's leaving preserved his pride and dignity. On the other, it punished everyone else. The other team involved and the officials stood around, not knowing what to do. Should they call the game off and replay it another night? Should the other team stand there and look foolish or walk off to the locker room? Should the fans go home without getting their money's worth or make their displeasure known? By using conflict avoidance, Knight effectively punished everyone present while restoring his own self-esteem.

Avoidance has this double effect. People who walk out on arguments are using double-edged avoidance. I lectured about this type of avoidance to a group of pastors several years ago. The next day, a young pastor rushed into class and exclaimed, "It happened to me last night. As we were discussing a change in our service, one of the elders got red in the face, stood up, and shouted, 'I'm leaving and not coming back! You never listen to me, anyway.'" Since this elder held an important office in the church, he knew full well that his leaving would be a disaster for the church, but that was only part of his intent. He truly was in conflict, and leaving the meeting was an effort to restore his self-esteem. If it cut both ways and also punished the group that put him in conflict, so much the better.

Threat Avoidance

Threat avoidance is a variation of double-edged avoidance. It can be recognized by the words, "If you . . . then I'll. . . ." The person in conflict is giving a forewarning that either his distress must be reduced or he'll retreat and leave the scene of conflict. Many times this serves to change the situation; sometimes it doesn't. A wife who tells her husband, "If you come home drunk again, I'll leave you" is using threat avoidance. On the surface, this sounds like logical problem solving, but most counselors agree that when a relationship reaches a point where threats to leave are made, the person doing the threatening is in conflict and fighting to retain his or her sense of dignity.

Threat avoidance is aggressive and effective as long as the second party believes the threats will be carried out. A woman who threatens to leave her husband every Saturday for twenty years is not very effective in changing the situation, any more than a mother who threatens to spank, but never does, is effective in changing her child's behavior.

On many occasions, just making the threat is enough to bolster a person's self-esteem to a satisfactory level. Sometimes appearing to be aggressive will reduce the person's conflict enough to allow him or her to remain in the situation. A gorilla beating on his chest in an aggressive manner is probably reducing his own tension while he tries to frighten off the intruder at the same time. This type of satisfaction will not result in any problems being solved, however.

Beat Them to the Punch

Another form of conflict avoidance is beating them to the punch. A humorous anecdote about a country preacher illustrates this type of avoidance. He had heard that a group within the church was planning to have him fired. At the close of the next service, one of the group was going to stand up and make a motion to fire the pastor. His motion would be supported by the other group members.

Since they were all men of high status in the church, the pastor was sure their motion would pass. Therefore, the next Sunday he stood behind the pulpit and stated, "Brothers and sisters, you can't fire me. I quit!"

People often quit before they're fired. It bolsters their self-esteem when they leave voluntarily, as painful as leaving may be. In some cases, a company will offer a person the chance to quit before he's fired, knowing he will leave happier and have a better chance of getting another decent job. This type of avoidance could be summed up by the phrase: Get out while the getting's good.

Again, the problem isn't solved by this type of avoidance, but the person who quits doesn't face the blow to his self-esteem that firing would bring, he is left with better feelings about himself, and he is out of conflict.

This Couldn't Be Happening to Me

This reaction to conflict is the most serious type of avoidance, since it involves mental blocking. Under great distress, our minds have the ability to protect themselves from massive emotional damage by blocking out emotions. We deny the facts of conflict, assert that everything's fine, and go on with our lives despite the fact that we're under distress that should disable us.

Children who have been physically or sexually abused often do not remember these events as adults. The damage is still there, but it takes extensive professional help to bring the actual events back into their memory so the mental and emotional damage can be dealt with. Men who have lived through combat often avoid their inner conflict the same way, as do survivors of natural disasters.

Even those of us who lead relatively safe, normal lives use this technique. "No, I'm not upset," we say when we really are upset. Then we go to our rooms, lock the door, and break down in private or sleep it off. At other times, we sit in front of the television set and watch children die of starvation, then get up and enjoy our favorite dinner. Are we hardhearted because of this? No. Our minds have simply blocked out our distress so we can continue to function.

It Don't Matter

It *don't matter* is another form of avoidance used in combat conflict situations. It's a more benign type of avoidance than mental blocking, but works the same way. The phrase comes from Flip Wilson's routine as pastor of The Church of What's Happening Now. After several outlandish statements about national and international situations. Pastor Flip would pronounce, "It don't *matter!*"

Some people put this into serious practice when they are in conflict. They simply withdraw and become numb. They protect themselves by no longer treating the issue or the relationship seriously. That which was causing them stress just doesn't matter when it becomes distressful.

Under problem-solving circumstances this might be seen as prioritizing issues. However, when a person is in conflict, it is a more drastic measure, designed primarily to restore self-esteem.

I had an aunt who would do this. Her behavior was so dramatic that you couldn't help but see her shift from involvement to indifference. For example, she would get into a discussion of where we were all going to go for dinner. She had strong opinons and would state them. Others might disagree or have alternative suggestions. The argument would become heated as several people tried to persuade the group to follow their preferences.

Then suddenly my aunt would withdraw. She would become silent, leave the room, return with her knitting, sit down, and say nothing. We would look at her and ask her what she wanted to do. "Who, me?" she would answer. "Do what you want. I've decided not to go to supper. It doesn't matter to me where you go." Try though we might to get her to go with us, she wouldn't do it. The family would go off and leave her, a bit subdued but knowing nothing would change her mind.

Later in the evening when we returned, she would be jovial, as if nothing had happened. It was a clear case of *it don't matter* avoidance that somehow restored her self-esteem.

You Don't Love Me, So I'm Leaving

A final type of conflict avoidance is *You don't love me, so I'm leaving.* In a sense this is a variation of *double-edged* avoidance, yet here there is little, if any, desire to punish others. Here the pain is genuinely so deep and the sense of deprivation so great that the person simply must get out of the situation or feel annihilated. Family feuds sometimes exemplify this type of avoidance.

In the movie *Moonstruck*, Cher's fiancé proposes marriage and tells her to invite his brother to the ceremony while he is away visiting his sick mother. She issues the invitation, but learns that the brothers have not spoken in five years because of an accident that resulted in the brother losing his hand as well as his girlfriend. He refuses to come to the wedding, preferring to safeguard his dignity by avoiding contact with the one he felt had wronged him.

Then there are real-life examples. Several years ago, a girl borrowed a car from her sister and wrecked it. She never paid her sister back for the cost of repairing the car, and her sister was furious. The situation became exaggerated over the years as the story was told and retold. Family members listened helplessly as each sister told her side of the story and tried to bolster her point of view and get members of the family to take sides.

On the occasion of a family reunion, the older sister who had loaned the car arrived early. She was dressed in her finest outfit and had brought special gifts for each family group. Obviously she was prepared for a wonderful day. However, the younger sister suddenly arrived at almost the same time as their parents. The older sister blew up. She could not understand why her younger sister had been invited when everyone knew how she felt about being around her. Because the sister arrived at the same time as their parents, the older sister assumed they had taken sides. She went back into the house, collected her gifts, and stormed out in a huff, shouting, "That does it! I'm never coming back to one of these reunions. This is the last time this family will ever see me!" Her clear intent was to maintain some sense of dignity in the midst of feeling unloved.

In every case of conflict avoidance, the goal is to regain some sense of self-esteem by retreating from the situation before being defeated. Such a retreat does reduce conflict, but never solves the problems behind the conflict.

Part III
The
Conventional Way

9

How to Handle a Leaky Roof
or
Calm Down

People in conflict do not all react the same way. While some react in a combat way, because they basically don't trust anyone but themselves, others have more faith in human nature and use the conventional way to reduce conflict. These people would wear sweatshirts urging others to be calm and trust the process.

People who think this way assume the social contract will work and justice will be done if they give it a chance. Although the term *social contract* has many meanings, its definition can be boiled down to one simple word: *manners*. There are certain acts that no mother approves of, and we all know more or less instinctively what they are. Our avoiding antisocial acts is the glue that holds society together and allows vastly different individuals to rub elbows with fairness and consideration for one another. The social contract assumes that normal people do not kill other people, run traffic lights, spit in public, or intentionally hurt another human being. Justice will be done, and no one will deprive us of life, liberty, and the pursuit of happiness.

Anyone who believes in the social contract tends to see other people as basically good and fair, not intentionally trying to frustrate or offend them. When people do cause them stress, conventional thinkers assume it's a mistake, a matter of misunderstanding that can be cleared up to everyone's satisfaction. These people believe that frustrating situations producing conflict are accidents that can be made right with justice and fairness to all.

This approach generally works, but it may fail when people become so upset that they stop believing in the social contract. In that case, they'll stew in their distress and won't give justice a chance. To be effective, the conventional way has to be seen as a two-step process: First you calm down, then you seek justice. You can't do it the other way around and have it work, and you can't leave out either step and still come out of conflict.

As an illustration of the conventional approach, take a young couple who were renting a top-floor apartment with a leaky roof. Time and time again, they asked their landlord to fix the leak, to no avail. As the weeks went on and more rain fell, the couple became more and more upset. Finally, when the rain leaked on their computer and damaged it, they became extremely distressed. "This is the last straw!" the young man told his wife. "We're not going to stand for this another minute. You'd think all the landlord wanted to do was take our rent and let us live in a slum. I don't know what we're going to do, but we're not going to let him get away with this!"

When this happened, the young man's wife was equally upset. They both stewed and mused over their dilemma from supper until bedtime, then lay awake talking about the problem until late at night. The next morning at breakfast, they continued to talk about the leak and their inability to get it fixed. "It's humiliating," the wife said, "to think that he cares so little for us that he lets us live with a leaky roof for two months! It's insulting. We've got to do something."

The husband looked up from his coffee. "I've got an idea. Let's meet at the health club this afternoon. After we exercise, we'll go out for some tacos, and when we come home, let's put on that relaxation tape and calm down. Let's not talk about it anymore until we're relaxed. There must be something we can do."

That evening, finally relaxed, they sat in their living room and discussed what should be done. They were still upset and felt humiliated and insulted, but they were finally calm. They telephoned the landlord, told him about the leak damaging their computer, demanded a meeting for the next day, and planned what they were going to say.

The next day, they laid out their concerns and firmly told the landlord they'd move if the leak wasn't fixed. They also expressed confidence that he would do the right thing. The landlord in turn told them about his frustration with three roofers who hadn't been able to find the leak. He said he understood their frustration and would get a fourth roofer over the next day for an estimate on reroofing the whole building.

The distress the young couple was feeling immediately diminished. They felt justified in demanding the meeting, and their pride in handling the situation made their self-esteem rise. By the time the meeting ended, they were no longer in distress.

This is a good example of the normal way to reduce conflict because it illustrates the two steps that are involved: calming down and demanding justice.

Calming down is the first step in reducing conflict by the conventional method. The couple with the leaky roof did this by exercising, going out for dinner, and listening to their relaxation tape.

Everyone in conflict is prone to catastrophic thinking. "Things are *never* going to get any better," we tell ourselves. "Nobody cares how we feel. We've got to do something fast!" People who think this way are sure that the process won't work, that they're doomed to a life without self-respect. They lose their basic trust in other humans and stay in conflict because they cannot reason or take appropriate action. Once they do calm down, they regain their trust in others and find ways to deal with their problems.

There are a number of ways to calm down and stop thinking in a catastrophic manner.

Relaxation

One way to calm down is to make use of the various relaxation techniques that are available today. When we perceive ourselves as being in danger, our bodies instinctively prepare us to defend ourselves. Blood rushes from the stomach to the brain, arms, and legs, preparing us to either fight or flee, and our eyes dilate so we can see our surroundings more clearly. This reaction, which is called the *general adaptation syndrome*, occurs whether the danger is an actual physical threat or a perceived one.

Our young soldier firing into the jungle is a good example of this physical response to danger. If he had been taking a pleasant stroll through the woods, he would have been relaxed and confident and might not even have been aware of the indistinct shape by the side of the trail. But he knew this was no peaceful walk in the woods; his senses were alert to any sign of danger, and he reacted instinctively to his first indication of the enemy. Through the ages, this adaptation syndrome has played an important part in the survival of the human race, and we should be thankful for it when there is real physical danger to be faced.

The young mother on the telephone was displaying the same reaction psychologically as she listened to her neighbor complain about little Tommy. She gripped the phone tightly in a hand that was beginning to sweat; her heart began beating more rapidly; her breathing became faster and more shallow; her face flushed in anger. She was alert to every nuance in her neighbor's voice, and when she heard the intimation that she was not a good mother, she was fully ready to fight back or run in defense.

The problem with this adaptation syndrome is that once our bodies have prepared us to defend ourselves, it's hard to tell whether we're reacting to the outside situation or to what our bodies are telling us to do. By relaxing, we regain control of our bodies and allow our brains to concentrate on the situation instead of on saving our lives.

There are many books and tapes available today to help us relax. If you have one on hand, it can be very effective. If you don't have one, there are two procedures you can use right away to relax your body, which will help you to avoid going into conflict, or facilitate your getting out of conflict.

The Quick Pick-Me-Up

This method takes less than thirty seconds and can be done throughout the day without anyone noticing. First, take in a deep breath. As you do, think to yourself, *Body, relax. Let go of tension, stress, and strain.* Then breathe out slowly, telling yourself over and over, *Clear mind, calm body.* Smile inwardly as you do this, to relax your facial muscles. Repeat this until you begin to feel your body relax and your mind clear.

Take Time to Relax

This next method takes twenty to thirty minutes and requires privacy. Lie down and close your eyes, taking several deep breaths. Slow, deep breathing is the single most important thing to do when you're in conflict. After you have taken several deep breaths, take one more as you tighten up all your body muscles. Scrunch up your toes, make a grimace on your face, tighten your hands into fists, and bend your legs and arms. Hold this tense position for as long as you can hold your breath, then exhale, relax your muscles, and breathe slowly and deeply for several minutes. Repeat this breathing, tensing, relaxing, and breathing sequence several times.

Pairing tension and relaxation in this manner forces your deep muscles to relax and helps you become aware of when you're tense and when you're relaxed. After you've repeated the sequence several times, continue to breathe deeply while you relax. Feel the tension flow out the tips of your toes and the ends of your fingers with a slightly warm, tingling sensation.

Now that your body is relaxed, it's no longer yelling at you, telling you that you're in danger. You can think clearly and deal with the problem at hand in a rational manner.

Defusing and Thought Control

The relaxation techniques discussed above calm your body; *defusing* and *thought stoppage* calm your mind and prevent catastrophic thinking. They allow you to realize you're not going to die from an insult, that your self-esteem is not in grave danger, and that your status is still intact.

Usually it's our subconscious that feels our self-esteem is under attack. Our conscious mind is more likely to be experiencing frustration. The couple with the leaky roof didn't consciously think about the danger to their self-esteem; they were frustrated by the negligence of their landlord. Our subconscious is capable of inducing catastrophic thinking even if our conscious mind is unaware of a threat to our self-esteem. It is important to be aware of how we really feel about a situation so we can then defuse our subconscious.

Defusing

Defusing is best done with a partner who begins the process by asking what you're feeling and thinking at the moment. Then the partner probes beneath your surface answer and emotions by asking, "If you weren't feeling that way, what would you be feeling? What's the feeling *beneath* your thoughts?" The partner should lead you down, layer by layer, like peeling an onion, until you finally admit what's bothering you on your subconscious level: "If I don't get this fixed, I feel I'll die psychologically. I don't know if I can face anyone else unless I do something about this."

Once you realize how you really feel, your partner should tell you, "Shut your eyes and imagine that the worst has happened. You've gotten no satisfaction, and things have gone from bad to worse. What's happening to you?"

At this point, most of us will admit we would survive. We lived through the worst possible scenario. Living through an imaginary trip like this defuses our feelings and calms us down. Once you have mastered this technique with the help of a partner, you'll be able to use it on your own.

Thought Stoppage

Thought stoppage is based on psychologist Albert Ellis's theory that there is a radical distinction between realistic and irrational thinking. He concludes that most of the times we think we're in distress and need to act drastically to survive, we're thinking irrationally, believing catastrophic thinking that tells us:

> "Everything has to go right for me to be successful."
> "Everybody has to like me, or I'm no good."
> "If I don't get my way, I can't respect myself."
> "When I fail at something, my world comes to an end."

He recommends that we take ourselves in hand and face these fanciful thoughts with reality. When we're thinking clearly, we know very well that we don't always have to succeed, be right, never fail, be loved by everyone, or get our way to have good self-esteem. Thinking we do throws us into a panic and puts us into distress, so we need to stop this type of thinking and be realistic.

Of course, this is easier said than done. I find it helpful to put a rubber band around my wrist when I'm in distress. When I have one of these irrational thoughts and feel I'm going into conflict, a snap of the rubber band reminds me to stop thinking in a catastrophic, irrational manner. It may sound silly, but it works.

Pulling Back

Pulling back is a procedure popularized by psychologist Carl Rogers. It involves recognizing that you have given to others something that belongs only to you — your self-respect — and then making a conscious effort to live by your own self-evaluation instead of the opinions of others. Rogers believes that we're all born whole, healthy, self-affirming, and complete in ourselves, but as we grow, our self-esteem becomes too dependent on what others think of us. Being dependent on the positions we hold (identity) or our reputations (status) gives others power over us — power that we should keep for ourselves. He recommends that we learn ways to reclaim our own goodness and a self-esteem that's based on our *own* evaluation of our worth.

Rogers suggests we find someone who knows us well and loves us. This person will provide us with an atmosphere of acceptance, understanding, warmth, and support that allows us to calm down, pull back from others' opinions about us, and reclaim our birthright. Having self-esteem that isn't dependent on what others think of us prevents us from going into conflict when they seem to disapprove of us.

Rogers recommends that psychotherapists provide this acceptance for their patients, but a friend, parent, or spouse can do the same thing for someone in conflict. It's important that this person doesn't make judgments or enter into the problem provoking the conflict; his or her job is simply to be accepting, understanding, and affirming. This unconditional love allows a person to regain her composure and realize she has self-worth no matter what's going on in her life.

Eugene Gendlin, in his book *Experiencing*, describes a way to regain your self-esteem on your own. He believes that as we grow, our minds become too aware of what others think of us, cutting us off from our naturally good feelings about our bodies and feelings. By calming ourselves and shutting our eyes, it's possible to relax our minds and reclaim our natural self-respect. This allows us to pull back from the evaluations of others and lets our minds and bodies function as they were intended to — on their own, without thought of what circumstances, or what other people, may bring.

Relaxation, defusing, thought stoppage, and pulling back, are conventional ways of reacting to conflict, that calm us down so we can stop thinking catastrophically and work on our problems logically. Our inner distress is reduced, and we come out of conflict prepared to trust the process and other people.

10

The Case of the Faulty Transmission
or
Trust the Process

Once people in conflict have calmed down, they're ready for the second step of handling conflict: trusting the process. It would be overly idealistic to think that people who were previously in distress totally trust the process of negotiation as soon as they calm down a little. Calming down makes reason possible, but deep hurts and feelings of low self-esteem can still plague a calm person. Yet, most of us are willing to enter into negotiation in hopes that things will work out and a fair decision will be reached. People who aren't as calm about the issue as they think they are may experience frustration and slip back into conflict while negotiation is going on. However, trying to smooth things out is always a matter of acting in good faith — even when we're not sure of the results.

While negotiating, it's also possible that the second party may go into conflict, throwing reason out the window and preventing any progress from being made.

Assuming both parties are calm and not in conflict, trusting the process usually works, as we all know from our daily lives.

What exactly is *the process?* How does it work? Generally, the process involves the natural give and take that goes on in most differences of opinion. For example, if you're in a supermarket checkout line and one item you're buying isn't marked with a price, a difference of opinion might arise between you and the cashier. You think the cost is $1.99, while the cashier thinks it's $2.99. To settle the matter, the cashier will usually ask another clerk for the correct price, consult a price list, or have the store's computer act as the third party. On receiving the correct price, one or the other of you will admit you were wrong and you'll go about your business.

The tacit assumption beneath this process is that no one's trying to cheat, and the difference of opinion can be resolved through an appeal to an unbiased judge who will act in a fair manner. The whole transaction is based on reason and logic rather than feelings or emotions. This type of give-and-take goes on all the time in our lives.

Sometimes this give-and-take doesn't work, though, and it's necessary to pursue a more formal means of reaching an agreement. We call this the *problem-solving method*, which is made up of specific steps to take when agreement is impossible to reach more informally. People who have been in conflict and then calmed themselves down may find these steps useful in restructuring the argument and preventing another impasse or another round of conflict.

Stating the Issue

The first step in the problem-solving process is being sure there is agreement on what the involved issue is. If the problem is so serious that someone went into conflict over it, you'd think everyone would be well aware of the issue, wouldn't you? But once we go into conflict, the issue isn't really the issue anymore — our hurt feelings and low self-esteem become the issue — and the real problem becomes so overburdened with emotions that it often falls by the wayside and is forgotten.

Agreeing on the issue itself is the first step toward reestablishing reason and objectivity as a basis for negotiation. Someone has to say, "Wait a minute. Before things got out of hand, weren't we trying to decide who is best qualified to be president?" Once everyone agrees on the issue, progress can be made.

This isn't always as easy as it sounds. Even when no one's in conflict, people often find it hard to agree on the issue. One person may see it as choosing a new president, while another wants to talk about revamping the whole electoral system, and another thinks the organization would be better off with no president! It'll take a little digging to get to the point where everyone agrees which points should be discussed, and in what order. It may be difficult to keep everyone on the same track while avoiding sending any member of the group into conflict.

Typing the Issue

Once the issue is defined to everyone's satisfaction, it needs to be *typed*. The question to be asked at this stage is, "What's the underlying concern of this issue?"

For example, say you had taken your car into the shop and the mechanic had to rebuild your transmission. Before your check has even cleared the bank, the transmission fails and you go back to the mechanic demanding he stand by his guarantee, at no cost to you.

The issue here is a dead car that you paid good money to have in working order. That's fairly easy to agree on. Your underlying concern is having a car that runs after you've paid money to have it fixed. If both you and the mechanic agree that his service was intended to provide you with reliable transportation — and why else would you have brought the car to him? — you can then sit down and discuss how this can be accomplished in a way that's fair to you both.

Clarifying the Differences

Once the issue has been defined and the underlying concerns are understood by all parties, it's a good idea to calmly review the various views on the subject. Having these differences agreed upon — even written down — is a good way to clear the chaff away from the issue.

When an argument deteriorates to the point that people go into conflict, extra feelings and issues become attached to the original problem. Like barnacles on a ship, they need to be chipped away before the ship will move the way it should. In longstanding relationships, people in conflict tend to gunnysack, or reach back into the past, pull out their old hurts and bitterness, and attach them to the present issue. If you went into conflict over the issue of your expensive but dead car, you may very well have reminded your mechanic of the time he put on your snow tires and tore a hole in the sidewall of a hundred-dollar tire. In retaliation, he may have mentioned that your last check bounced higher than the torn tire. Even if both accusations are true, neither is part of the transmission problem. The accusations need to be cleared away from the present issue before you can agree on how to fix that transmission.

Searching for New Solutions

If someone goes into conflict during an argument the situation has probably already reached an impasse and the opportunity for reaching a solution that's completely agreeable to all is gone. Now it's time to work toward saving face for everyone, rather than thinking complete agreement is still possible. Compromise is in order.

Looking for new solutions should reflect a desire to negotiate and to admit that neither side was completely right. This is hard to do because passionately held opinions involve people's pride and are often hard to give up. Those who went into conflict and then calmed down enough to reenter the process will need to admit that they were not totally right. They're the ones who disturbed the negotiations in the first place and reacted emotionally while the others remained rational. They probably owe the other parties an apology and will have to bend a little if they want to see the problem solved. Then they all can get down to the business of deciding what's necessary to make everyone more or less happy.

Once everyone's back on an even keel and willing to give a little, brainstorming new solutions to the problem becomes critical. The old solutions were not acceptable to everyone, but they aren't the only solutions available. Most problems can be solved in a variety of ways, one of which will be acceptable to everyone involved. Brainstorming always carries the presumption that everyone has good ideas. It provides the chance to compromise and find solutions that allow everyone to save face. Self-esteem is always an issue for everyone involved, so saving face cannot be shrugged off as unimportant or a side issue. At this point, there can be no winners and no losers, or there will be no solution.

Negotiation

If the process has gotten this far, finding a solution through negotiation is almost a sure thing. Everyone will have to give up a pet point or two, and no one will get everything he wants, but all concerned will feel they've been treated fairly and gotten what they deserved. When this happens, those who were in distress will come out of conflict.

While I have great faith in this problem-solving process, there are two cautions to be considered. First, it may be a little too idealistic about people, who may not be as well-meaning as the approach assumes they are. Sometimes you end up dealing with a stinker whose only aim is to win at all costs. Even if both parties are well-meaning, one may still be in conflict and less willing to negotiate than the other. The process works best when both parties are at the same place psychologically.

The second caution to consider is that some situations are more amenable to compromise than others. Negotiating a guarantee on a repaired transmission is possible, but sometimes the issue requires an either/or decision, with no room for compromise. A math student talking with a professor about his grade on a test got either the right answer to a problem or the wrong answer, and there's no room for compromise. If there is no middle ground, the conventional way to reduce conflict is under a handicap.

An Example

I once consulted on a church situation that illustrates the way the conventional method works. In this situation, a beloved pastor had been accused of an act that could not be forgiven or overlooked by the congregation. The church board considered the accusations and fired the pastor very quickly, believing they needed to act before the matter was made public. Another group in the church felt differently. The pastor was their longtime friend, and they simply could not believe he had done such a thing. They felt the board had acted too hastily and had not given the pastor a chance to defend himself.

The two groups engaged in heated discussions. Much telephoning and gossip ensued, and many people threatened to leave the church. Before long, the whole congregation was in conflict. A concerned committee composed of people from both sides asked me to help them deal with the issue.

I used the conventional way of reducing conflict in the church. I met separately with both sides, listening carefully and nonjudgmentally. Many feelings of outrage and hurt surfaced. It was obvious that this situation was only the catalyst for the reemergence of many old controversies. I encouraged them to calm down and try to reduce the conflict they were feeling, then I invited them to meet together with me.

At the meeting, I led them through the problem-solving steps. We agreed that the issue was whether the minister should have been fired before being given the chance to plead his case. This statement of the issue was printed in big letters on newsprint, and everyone agreed that this was the issue.

We then tried to type the issue. Was this a matter of ways, means, or ends? Since by the time I was called in it was apparent that the minister was guilty of the accusations, everyone agreed this was a matter of ways. By this time, even those members who deeply appreciated the past service of the minister knew he had to be fired. However, they still felt his long service with the church should have dictated a more gentle firing.

Next we tried to see if we could discover some new solution to the problem. Since by the time of the meeting the minister had been gone for six months, going back and finding a new way to fire him was impossible. So we searched for a way to assuage the feelings of those who were hurt by the process. At the same time, we sought understanding for the dilemma the members of the church board felt they were in when they made their decision.

We discovered a middle-of-the-road solution that fully satisfied no one, but partially satisfied everyone. The church board issued an apology and an explanation. This statement honored the past service of the minister and communicated genuine respect and understanding for those who had risen up in his defense. The board apologized for the quickness with which it had acted, but asked for understanding from the church at large because of the situation it faced.

Finally we negotiated a plan of action. Not only did the board set down some guidelines for what it would do in the future, to assure more consensus for its actions in times of serious problems, but it planned a celebration of reconciliation to which all parties were invited. The celebration included a covered-dish supper, statements by both sides, Holy Communion, and an evening of fun and games.

I feel this illustrates what can be done when goodwill is shared and members of both sides calm down enough to trust the process. When I last heard from this church, it was healthy and strong. Little residue of the difficulties they went through seemed to remain.

Part IV
The
Christian Way

11

The Four R's

or

The Christian Way to Reduce Conflict

The Christian way to reduce conflict is totally different from the combat and conventional ways, both of which treat conflict as the result of external influences. The combative person goes into conflict when she feels rejected by others; the conventional person, when he feels misunderstood. Both deal with problems caused either intentionally or accidentally by other people. Coping with the problems involves dealing directly with other people from the beginning, since their self-esteem is directly related to others' perceptions of them.

The Christian way sees conflict as an internal, personal problem that arises when Christians temporarily forget who they are and on what their self-esteem truly rests. Instead of being dependent on others for their self-esteem, Christians are dependent on God's love for them — something no one can take away or endanger. Therefore, the first step in reducing conflict the Christian way involves remembering God's love for, and acceptance of us. If God loves us and accepts us as we are, how can mere humans endanger our self-esteem? It doesn't come from them in the first place, and they can't affect God's feelings for us. Our self-esteem is secure, no matter what people may think of us!

Remember the story of the time I went into conflict over mowing the grass with no help from my family? Had I chosen the Christian way to reduce my conflict, I would have stopped and remembered what I'd forgotten: My self-worth was not dependent on whether or not people helped me mow the lawn. Neither was my identity a function of the fact that I was a homeowner, father of three sons, professor, or part-time gardener. My status does not depend on my being a good provider, indulgent father, skilled teacher, or fast grass cutter. I would have remembered that my self-esteem is based on something that lies beneath my roles and status.

Harvard psychologist Gordon Allport made this same point while writing about the meaning of personality. The Greek word *personae*, which lies at the core of our word *personality*, originally referred to dramatic actors who often played several parts in one play. On one hand, *personae* meant the roles the actors played in a given scene. On the other hand, it also meant the actors themselves — the people beneath the roles.

Who am I? Am I the roles I'm playing at any given moment or the person beneath the roles? The Christian way of reducing conflict says you are the person beneath the roles you play. In fact, you are who you are, even when you're not playing any role. Actors are still persons no matter who they are on stage. They remain the same person, and just like the rest of us, they probably wonder sometimes how people would feel about them if they really knew them.

Christians know exactly how God feels about them, in spite of the fact that He knows them totally and completely. "O Lord, thou hast searched me, and known me. Thou knowest my downsitting and mine uprising, thou understandest my thought afar off . . . For there is not a word in my tongue, but, lo, O Lord, thou knowest it altogether" (Psalms 139:1, 2, 4 KJV). Regardless of how others feel about us, God loves us. Our self-esteem is totally secure in His arms. It is not based on our deeds or our basic goodness, either. It's based on the fact that God loves us apart from our identities, our reputations, or our actions. Sins and all, God accepts us with unconditional love when we accept Him in our hearts. This is the Good News of the Gospel: "For by grace are ye saved through faith; and that not of yourselves: it is the gift of God: Not of works, lest any man should boast" (Ephesians 2:8, 9 KJV).

Our problem when we go into conflict is that we have forgotten this eternal and never-changing truth. We need to remember these words "For God so loved the world that he gave his only Son, that whoever believes in him should not perish but have eternal life" (John 3:16).

When we are in conflict, we forget this and think we're about to die psychologically. We feel humilated, embarrassed, threatened, and anxious. But, someone who has been promised eternal life doesn't ever have to doubt her own self-worth! Our lives are not up for grabs or susceptible to life's circumstances. "I came that they may have life, and have it abundantly" (John 10:10). We won't go into conflict as long as we remember Jesus' love for us.

In addition, the Bible tells us: "For God did not send his Son into the world to be its Judge, but to be its savior" (John 3:17 TEV). We are saved, not judged. We are saved from giving our self-esteem into the hands of others. We are saved from guilt. We are saved from conflict.

The Christian way to reduce conflict includes four steps: remember, reaffirm, repent, and reassert.

Remember

Remember Calvary. We do this by recollecting or reading the words of the Bible. Those who want to use the Christian model should carry a New Testament with them, so that when they go into conflict they can take a moment to read such passages of Scripture as John 3:16, 17 or Luke 12:22-28. Another helpful passage would be:

> But God has shown us how much he loves us —it was while we were still sinners that Christ died for us! By his death we are now put right with God; how much more, then, will we be saved by him from God's anger! We were God's enemies,

but he made us his friends through the death of his Son. Now that we are God's friends, how much more will we be saved by Christ's life! But that is not all; we rejoice because of what God has done through our Lord Jesus Christ, who has now made us God's friends.

Romans 5:8-11 TEV

Reading these passages should quiet our fears, calm our anxieties, reduce our conflict, and restore our self-esteem. However, it doesn't always work that way. In fact, it *rarely* works that way. As the old saying goes, "Saying doesn't make it so and reading doesn't make it true." We don't always act on what we know, in other words.

This is such a common human trait that even Paul struggled with it. As he said:

We know that the Law is spiritual; but I am a mortal man, sold as a slave to sin. I do not understand what I do; for I don't do what I would like to do, but instead I do what I hate. Since what I do is what I don't want to do, this shows that I agree that the Law is right. So I am not really the one who does this thing; rather it is the sin that lives in me. I know that good does not live in me — that is, in my human nature. For even though the desire to do good is in me, I am not able to do it. I don't do the good I want to do; instead, I do the evil that I do not want to do . . . My inner being delights in the law of God. But I see a different law at work in my body — a law that fights against the law which my mind approves of . . . This, then, is my condition: on my own I can serve God's law only with my mind, while my human nature serves the law of sin.

Romans 7:14-19, 22, 23, 25 TEV

We are all like Paul. Just remembering the fact of our salvation isn't enough to make us act as we should. If we think it is, we'll only fall back into conflict with the slightest stress. I well remember this happening to me one time when I was in conflict. I read the Scripture and felt that I had needlessly become distressed. I felt so good about myself that I tried to go right back to the person whose rejection had put me into conflict, but when he didn't react as I had hoped he would, I plunged back into conflict — even more distressed than I had been before! This illustrates the fact that we need to do more than just remember God's love for us.

Reaffirm

We need to move to the second step in the Christian way to reduce conflict: reaffirmation. Reaffirmation means making sure that the truth of God's love for us is deeper than *head knowledge*. These truths need to be in our very hearts. Only when God's love becomes a personal truth for us by seeping down to our innermost being can it work for us in the world. As the Scripture states, "For as he thinketh in his heart, so is he" (Proverbs 23:7 KJV).

How do we reaffirm God's love for us? The traditional method is through prayer. Prayer is a way of tuning out distractions while we thank God for all He's done for us and ask Him to make the truth of Scripture come alive in our hearts. Through prayer, head knowledge becomes heart knowledge, insight becomes healing, truth becomes reality.

Although this sounds relatively easy, making the transition from remembering to reaffirmation is not a simple task. John Wesley was an Anglican priest for many years before he felt in his heart that the gospel he had been preaching to others, was also true for himself. He wrote that his heart was strangely warmed, and he knew his sins were forgiven after attending a Moravian prayer meeting on Aldersgate Street in London on May 23, 1738 — over a decade after he had been ordained to the ministry!

It doesn't usually take quite that long, but it does take time, and it's a process Christians must go through before they can use the Christian way to reduce conflict effectively. Most people using this system find that they need to get away from the stressful situation that provoked the problem, and spend some time alone in reading and prayer before they really and truly experience release from their panic. Getting away from the situation may not always be possible, but a break of a few minutes can always be arranged in any discussion. Once you're safely alone, you can take out your New Testament, read the passages that tell of God's love, spend some time in prayer, and then return to the battleground without anyone being the wiser.

Of course it's even better to get away from the situation entirely and spend a full morning or afternoon in reflection and prayer. There's no doubt that circumstances can be distracting and threatening, and it's difficult to quiet down and stop worrying without a little time alone.

Repent

Once Christians calm down, they need to repent, to ask forgiveness of God for their sins. But what sins are involved in going into conflict?

Since Christians only go into conflict when they forget who they are and don't remember that their self-esteem is based on God's unconditional love for them, the act of forgetting in itself needs to be forgiven. Going into conflict is *our* problem, not God's. God was standing there by the door all day, waiting for us to hear Him knocking and let Him back into our hearts, but in our distress, we forgot He was there and refused Him entry. Refusing God's love is a sin that must be repented of. Allowing ourselves to become anxious and desperate was our sin.

Do we need to repent for asserting ourselves? No! God put us on earth to be creative, to have opinions, to take stands, to argue our convictions, and to attempt to convince others of our point of view. There's no need to repent for taking part in a controversy, even if we become angry and argumentative in the process. Anger isn't the problem; what we do with our anger is.

Wrath, on the other hand, does need to be repented of. When we let anger turn to wrath, we become embroiled in hatred, bitterness, revenge, and ill will. We discount the value of others who are important before God, treat them in an un-Christian manner, and insult their Creator. Scripture commands us to deal with wrath as soon as it appears: "Be angry, but do not sin, do not let the sun go down on your anger, and give no opportunity to the devil" (Ephesians 4:26, 27).

We should repent of bitter thoughts and vengeful actions we take when we are in conflict. Although it's very human to let our anger become wrath and to let our wrath turn to bitterness and retaliation, such feelings cannot be tolerated when we reenter the stressful situation. The Sermon on the Mount states this boldly when it declares:

> You have heard that people were told in the past, "Do not commit murder; anyone who does will be brought to trial." But now I tell you: whoever is angry with his brother will be brought to trial, whoever calls his brother "You good-for-nothing!" will be brought before the Council, and whoever calls his brother a worthless fool will be in danger of going to the fire of hell.
>
> Matthew 5:21, 22 TEV

There is a scriptural and psychological reason for repenting of our ill will toward others. Since God loves everyone, regardless of what they have done, it would be anathema for those who remember and reaffirm

His love to indulge in a disparaging, hateful discounting of those whom God has declared precious! We cannot claim for ourselves what we deny others. If we are loved in spite of our sins, then so are they.

The psychological reason for repenting of our wrath is that we will be unable to negotiate with those whose motives we doubt and whose value we negate. Part of repentance involves seeing the situation from their point of view as well as accepting their worth as human beings.

This leads to a third reason for repentance: overcommitment to our own point of view. We do not need to repent for asserting our opinion or for trying to persuade others to support us, but when we are on that dangerous line between stress and distress, we often become overcommitted to our particular viewpoint. We become so ego involved in convincing others and having them support our position that we become desperately committed to one side of the argument.

If we do not repent of this overcommitment and think about the real issues, we will be stubbornly invested in one viewpoint when we go back into the situation. Repenting of overcommitment frees us from being too ego involved and allows us to consider new options for resolving the problem. No one is perfect; God does not ask us to be, and we are not saved by works, as Scripture reminds us. There is no sin in being wrong and admitting it!

Reassertion

Remembering, reaffirming, and repenting are essentially private acts done apart from others. They calm us down, restore our self-esteem, and prepare us to re-enter the argument ready to find a fair solution. The danger is that we will be tempted to stop right here and not go back into the disagreement. After all, if God loves us apart from what we've done, are doing, or will do, why bother to do anything? Stopping here often leads Christians into lethargy and withdrawal from the world. This is pseudo piety. Truly religious people always go back into the world.

Some might look back on the situation and correctly decide it was unimportant and not worth pursuing now that they're calm and collected. It's true that many of the stress situations that distress us don't matter all that much once we've stepped back from them. Prioritizing and keeping ourselves from becoming ego involved in a lot of unnecessary battles is a good thing, on some occasions.

For example, I plan to retire in a few years. Once I began to think about ending my career, I became aware that I was having some very childish fears. I felt ambivalent as I saw younger staff members take on some of my former responsibilities. On the one hand, they were making life easier for me and I was glad about it. On the other, those were *my* jobs, I was ego involved with them, and I was reluctant to let go of them. I needed to sit down and determine my priorities without withdrawing completely from campus life as though it didn't matter to me anymore.

This type of evaluation is useful and necessary in life, however, there are many times when withdrawal is not good. Often we need to go back to the disagreement and straighten things out, not withdraw from it. What happens in the world is important to God. He created the world, chose the Hebrews as His people, gave them the Ten Commandments, sent the prophets, sent Jesus into the world to save it, gave us the Holy Spirit for guidance, and promised to come back one day to rule the world Himself. Are these the actions of a God who doesn't care what goes on down here? The Christian faith is firmly wedded to *action*, not withdrawal from the world. Once Christians have reduced their conflict through remembering, reaffirming, and repenting, they have a duty to reenter situations through reassertion.

Church people are often the worst offenders when it comes to avoiding reassertion. They prefer to avoid controversy. In one case, a pastor asked a woman to assume some responsibilities for the church school. The church school superintendent became offended because she thought the other woman was being asked to take over some of her duties and the pastor had not talked with her before making the appointment. She resigned her position and left the church in conflict. No amount of persuasion or apology could change her mind. When she was asked why she would not reconsider, she replied, "I think Christians should be peacemakers. It's over, and it just isn't important enough for me to come back."

In this case, she was mistaken. Issues are not settled when people withdraw from each other. In fact, the conflict has only been partially reduced if people don't come together and try to work out their differences.

Other people set their goals too high and use this as a reason to avoid reassertion. They don't feel they can live up to Jesus' command to forgive completely, and perhaps they can't, but that's no reason to give up on the world.

Once the decision has been made to reenter the situation, what are the ground rules for a Christian? What are the goals of reassertion?

At the bare minimum, it's important for the Christian to remember the difference between assertion and aggression. Since disparagement and the discounting of others has been confessed in the repentance step, neither is admissable in reassertion. There must be no attempts at retaliation. Christians are free to state their opinions forcefully as long as they give others the same right. By following these simple guidelines, a person may reenter the issue, receive a fair hearing, and take part in negotiating a fair decision. Even if there are still some hard feelings floating around, conflict can be avoided if these rules are followed.

The optimum goal of reassertion goes even further and involves attempts at peacemaking. Ideally, peacemaking leads to agreement on how to solve the distressful problem and still be able to work together in the future. If peacemaking is successful, the people involved actually emerge from the situation trusting each other more.

The Christian way of reducing conflict is a difficult way, but it works. It does so because it has the potential for reuniting people while admitting there are difficulties to be overcome. Finally, through the Good News of the Gospel, the Christian approach takes conflict into the heart of God's will and forgives sin as well as demands action.

Part V
Practical Conflict Reduction

12

The Baggage Porter's Method
or
Good, Better, Best

As we've seen, there are three basic ways to reduce conflict — the combat, conventional, and Christian way. Which one is the best? To help us decide, let's use three criteria: function, style, and value.

Function

All three methods work. They all reduce distress to stress, although they do it in radically different ways. The combat way involves fighting for your rights, surrendering, avoiding, or denying the fact that you're in conflict — all of which will reduce your stress. By helping you calm down, affirm yourself, trust the process, and renegotiate, the conventional way also effectively reduces distress. The Christian way works by reminding you of God's love for you and your self-worth, which leads to repentance and reassurance.

Even though all three ways work, there's no guarantee that any of them will produce lasting results, however. Remember, we go into and out of conflict rapidly and often, for various reasons and to various degrees. Although it's not necessary to go into conflict, it does seem inevitable. Christians forget who they are and slip over the line between stress and distress time and again. Likewise, the conventional way has to be used over and over again as new crises arise. Probably the best proof that no method is guaranteed to last is the ease with which we slip into crisis and find ourselves fighting, surrendering, or retreating — using the combat way time after time throughout our lives. Although all three systems will work in a given situation, none of them has the advantage of providing a permanent "cure" for conflict.

When we're looking for fast relief, though, it's no contest. The combat method works the fastest. Nobody likes a fight, and many people will give in or retreat when another person attacks through the combat method. If you don't want to attack, surrendering is even quicker, providing instant approval, pity, or acceptance. Retreating from the scene or denying you're frustrated will also provide instant relief from conflict. There's no doubt that the conventional and Christian ways take more time to reduce conflict than the combat way.

On the other hand, the combat way rules out the possibility of real problem solving and the restoration of relationships. If you attack, you run the risk of losing a friend; if you run, you've allowed the problem to change your relationship. No true progress can be made through the combat system, because someone is always hurt by it.

The conventional way allows for problem solving and the continuation of the relationship by assuming that people are basically fair and things can be worked out to everyone's satisfaction.

The Christian approach assumes that people are basically evil and sinful, but that God forgives and redeems them. People who use the Christian system want to work things out to the glory of God and maintain their relationship with one another.

The technique you use when in conflict will depend on what you need the most at the moment — instant relief or a continuing relationship with the other person. It's a good idea to keep your goals in mind when making your choice of action. Unfortunately, a person in conflict isn't very reasonable, and it may take a good deal of willpower to hold your tongue long enough to decide between winning the battle or keeping a friend.

Style

Style involves your natural tendencies, the types of action and reaction you're most comfortable with. Some people will attack without thinking when in conflict; others will back off. What you feel toward people and how you were brought up affect your natural style and help determine which of the three ways of reducing conflict you'll employ.

Those of us in the West tend to trust others. Western mothers strive to raise children who have confidence in themselves, cooperate with others, and trust authorities enough to want to please them. The motherly admonition to stop, look, and listen before crossing a street implies that if you get hit, it's because you weren't careful enough, not because the driver was aiming at you. Most of us are brought up to believe this is a just world, filled with people who are basically fair and good-natured, not evil, which is the conventional system's outlook on life.

Then we grow up and leave our mothers. Things happen that shake our confidence in justice. We read history and learn about the myriad ways that people can be and are inhumane to others. Many of us have personal experiences that shake our faith in others' basic goodness, and we eventually begin to doubt our conventional assumptions.

I can remember some of my own disillusionment as I grew up in Alabama. By the time I was in my late teens, I had become deeply remorseful of the times I had driven through the black section of town and exploded cherry bombs in front of people living there. I had become aware of the discriminatory laws against blacks, and I became extremely suspicious of all elected officials. The first time I took the Minnesota Multiphasic Personality Test in graduate school, I was afraid that my experiences in fighting for racial justice would make me test as a paranoid personality!

By the time I was an adult, my trust in the conventional method of reducing conflict had been severely shaken, and the combat approach felt more normal to me. Now, when it comes to conflict, I tend to be a tank commander. I arm myself for battle and ride out to annihilate anyone in my way. I'm not proud of this, but combat thinking is what comes naturally to me.

Of the three ways of reducing conflict, the Christian way is the most unnatural, since we base our behavior more on things we can see than on those we can't. As the soldier in the film *The Robe* concluded, "Since the God of the Christians has not yet come, in the meantime I will serve Rome." Most of us are like that, even if we've had a personal experience with God and worship Him. In daily life, there's a strong temptation to "serve Rome."

Although I strongly believe the Christian way will work and is the most realistic approach, I also believe it's the toughest approach to use. You have to stop and remind yourself of its power, then force yourself to use it. Jesus knew we would forget spiritual truths in the face of everyday life, so He established the rite of communion: "This do in remembrance of me." When it comes to style, the Christian way is the least likely to be practiced out of habit.

Virtue

The combat, conventional, and Christian ways will all reduce conflict, even though they naturally appeal to different types of people. But which of them is the most virtuous?

Virtue is often confused with function, but what works best isn't necessarily virtuous. When we ask which method is the best to use, we mean which has the greatest merit, which has the most worth, which is truest to our ideals.

The Christian way is clearly the most virtuous. It doesn't assume that people will act lovingly toward one another, but it does affirm them and offer them a chance for redemption from their selfishness. It makes collaboration, problem solving, and a better world possible.

The combat approach makes no provision for collaboration and assumes self-centeredness is a fact of life. The conventional approach, while assuming people can work together, has no goal higher than live and let live.

Late in the seventeenth century, Sir Isaac Newton and his colleagues founded the Royal Society of Science to "investigate the laws of nature for the glory of God and the relief of human suffering." For Christians, conflict reduction has the same goals: the glory of God and the alleviation of human suffering. The Christian way is the only one of the three that is based on a transempirical, supernatural set of principles. It's the only one that assumes a reality above and beyond ourselves that is personal and caring — a God who has redeemed His creation and has a plan for it. Furthermore, Christians assume that God is willing and able to help them in their daily lives.

The Christian way combines the hope of the conventional way with the reality of the combat way. Christians know that God created humans to live together in love and peace, but that this is still more a hope than a reality. They admit that people are sinfully preoccupied with survival and alienated from one another. Christians, however, are convinced that God hasn't given up on us, that He still loves us and wants to welcome us back, and that conflict reduction is possible when people are secure in God's love for them.

The Christian way and how it reduces conflict are exemplified in this story of a baggage porter at Chicago's O'Hare airport who was accused of not handling a traveler's bag with enough care. The porter apologized and continued about his work while the traveler huffed and puffed at him. Insisting on reporting the porter, the traveler left him a fifty-cent tip for three bags and stalked off. The next person in line asked the porter, "How can you stand there and take that?"

The porter answered, "I just hum to myself, 'Pass me not, O gentle Savior. Hear my humble cry. While on others Thou art calling, do not pass me by.' This reminds me of what life is really all about. It helps me not to fight back when things like that occur."

Some people would say the porter was denying his conflict by saying it wasn't important, but not all things are equally important. In this case, the porter's relationship with Christ was more important to him than his feelings of being insulted. He reminded himself of something even more important for his self-esteem, and remembering this, his conflict was reduced.

So all three approaches to reducing conflict do work. The combat approach comes most naturally to us, but the Christian way is inherently the most virtuous of the three. Which will you use the next time you're in conflict?

13

Buster, the Very Wet Terrier
or
Conflict Prevention

So far, we've been discussing how to get out of conflict. We should also consider how to *stay out* of conflict.

I can remember how our cute — but very wet — terrier, Buster, would slip into the house when it was raining. My mother would chase him around the kitchen while he scampered back and forth trying to avoid her grasp. To us, it was an amusing race, but she would eventually catch him, open the back door, and push him out, shouting, "Now you get out — and stay out!" Although Buster would lower his head, tuck his tail, and look back at us with soulful eyes, his remorse would last only a short time, and he would sneak back into the kitchen when we least expected it.

It's the same with our tendency to go back into conflict. Like a dog sneaking into the kitchen, conflict will steal back into our lives if we don't take measures to prevent it. The goal of conflict prevention is identical to my mother's command to Buster: Get out and stay out!

Of course, it would be better if we'd never gone into conflict in the first place. Humans are not constructed so that they *must* go into conflict; it's not necessary to become distressed and go into conflict to be a human being. We tend to think that what we observe is the way things really are, and if we observe that most people go into conflict, we tend to think that conflict is an instinctive, natural characteristic of humans. I'm convinced this isn't true.

Stress from frustration is part of the structure of life, since we are all independent thinkers who see things differently. It is possible, though, for us to settle our differences without getting stressed-out and going into conflict. I want to hold out the hope and possibility that life can be lived totally conflict free.

Conflict prevention therefore has a double focus: staying out of conflict after a conflict has been resolved, and never going into it in the first place. Staying out of conflict after being in conflict is like keeping your blood pressure down after the doctor has lowered it through diet, exercise, and medicine. Never going into conflict in the first place is similar to practicing good health habits and preventing your blood pressure from ever getting dangerously high. The four ways you can prevent conflict are: deterrence, detection, detainment, and declaration.

Deterrence

Deterrence is similar to taking a detour. We've all come to detour signs when traveling. They usually mean the road is being repaired, or a mudslide has occurred, or a bridge has been washed out. To keep from running into trouble or not reaching our destination, we generally take the detour. But, not all of the time.

I can remember driving a back road to a scenic historical sight in Kentucky and coming to a detour sign. I didn't want to take it, because we were near our destination and it would mean an extra thirty miles of driving. "Besides," I reasoned, "if the bridge is out, the ferry will be running." My wife wasn't so sure about that and preferred the extra thirty miles, but I was behind the wheel, so we continued on until we came to the washed-out bridge and nonoperating ferry! Not only did we have to drive the extra thirty miles, we also had to backtrack to find the detour.

Conflict prevention by deterrence works the same way as a detour sign. It will take extra time to avoid going into conflict, but never as much as it would take to get out of conflict.

What are some of the techniques for detouring around distress? According to Eugene Gendlin, when we become distressed, it's because we've separated our minds from our bodies. Our minds become overly concerned with other people's opinions of us, and we forget our own goodness. By keeping our minds in contact with our bodies, we can experience our wholeness and goodness, thus avoiding the anxiety that comes from giving our self-esteem away to others.

By practicing Gendlin's "experiencing" daily, we can prepare ourselves for the day's frustrations. Then when we do experience stress we can remain calm, knowing that we are sound, whole, and worthy just because we are who we are.

Gendlin told the story of a woman who was greatly threatened by her mother-in-law. On the way to visit her one day, the young woman left the freeway and called Dr. Gendlin from a pay telephone because she was in a state of panic and anxiety. He instructed her to put the telephone receiver down and reexperience her wholeness. In a few minutes she came back on the line and told him she felt okay again.

To "experience," you close your eyes and imagine that the block separating your mind from your body is slowly melting away. This block is mentally located in the throat, so that swallowing as you imagine the block melting lets the connection be made once again. As the block melts, the body and mind begin to flow together. Thoughts flow to all parts of the body — to the tips of the fingers and the ends of the toes. In turn, the body sends messages to the brain. The body/mind hums, to coin a phrase, and a warmth comes over all your being. You feel a sense of wholeness and goodness again.

This technique is often combined with daily self-messages that people can say to themselves while standing in front of a mirror: "This is me, and I'm good", "I am who I am, and I like myself," and so forth.

In this regard, Christians have special resources for deterring conflict. We believe the words of God which tell us He "saw every thing that he had made, and, behold, it was very good" (Genesis 1:31 KJV). Christians can say everything Gendlin's people can say, and more.

They are not only good because they can unite their minds and bodies, but because they are part of God's good creation. They know God loves them and His love is not dependent on their goodness. God loves them even when they aren't good.

Be still, and know that I am God. . . .

Psalms 46:10

The Lord is my shepherd; I shall not want.

Psalms 23:1

And God's peace, which is far beyond human understanding, will keep your hearts and minds safe, in union with Christ Jesus.

Philippians 4:7 TEV

But they who wait for the Lord shall renew their strength, they shall mount up with wings like eagles; they shall run and not be weary, they shall walk and not faint.

Isaiah 40:31

This is the day which the Lord has made; let us rejoice and be glad in it.

Psalms 118:24

When I consider thy heavens, the work of thy fingers, the moon and the stars, which thou hast ordained; What is man, that thou art mindful of him? and the son of man, that thou visitest him? For thou has made him a little lower than the

> angels, and hast crowned him with glory and honour. Thou madest him to have dominion over the works of thy hands; thou hast put all things under his feet.
>
> Psalms 8:3-6 KJV

These are just a few Scripture verses Christians can use to build up their self-esteem and detour around the storms of distress. There are two other resources that can be used on a daily basis to strengthen your resolve to keep from going into distress: prayer and daily devotions.

Daily prayer used this way should include several components: thanksgiving for God's love; confession of the temptation to forget that His love is the true basis for self-esteem; acceptance of His love; asking God to help you stay out of conflict; repentance for any ill will toward others; and resolution to make your daily tasks show forth God's love to others and help make the world a better place in which to live.

Devotions can include religious literature, but they should also include some systematic reading from the Bible. This type of Bible reading is different from recalling the affirmations of truth noted above. There are many guides for such reading, but one that has stood the test of time is the Lectionary that can be found in such volumes as *The Book of Common Prayer* of the Episcopal Church, which has daily readings from the Psalms, the Old Testament, the New Testament Epistles, and the Gospels. Another fruitful guide is *The One Year Bible* published by Tyndale Press, which includes Old and

New Testament readings, a Psalm, and a portion of Proverbs for each day.

Think of these daily readings as seeds planted in your subconscious. Don't try to force them into some applied truth for your affairs on a given day. If they have immediate meaning for your day, that's fine, but usually they'll be general truths that function in your subconscious to stabilize you when stress arises, reminding you that your identity and status are secure.

A final word about conflict prevention through deterrence: It will take time. All exercise takes time, but the time will be well spent.

Detection

To prevent conflict through detection, you need to become aware of the early warning signs that you or someone else is moving from stress to distress. Subtle but significant changes occur almost automatically when we move toward conflict.

We should all be aware of our personal conflict histories, clearly identifying the times, places, and people that have distressed us in the past, and then, be on the lookout for these situations in our present lives. I'm vulnerable to conflict when I'm around women in their fifties because of my experience with my mother when she was that age. Becoming aware of your vulnerabilities can make you more vigilant, so you can avoid or prepare for these encounters.

In addition, we should all understand our unique physiological responses as we move from stress to distress. Our bodies react differently as we go into distress, our autonomic nervous systems prepare our bodies for battle. Realizing that you experience burning eyes, tightness in the stomach, sweating palms, a red face, a pain in the back, or whatever, is an important first step in becoming a good conflict detective. These early warning signs can be handled through quick muscle relaxation, taking a break from the situation, by "experiencing," or by calming yourself down through Christian resources. Stopping yourself from going into conflict is much more difficult later in the process.

It's also helpful to understand how others behave when they're about to go into conflict. Since we know that nothing can be accomplished when people are in conflict, we can try to defuse the situation or help them regain their self-esteem if we're sensitive to the signs of conflict in others. The ancient Roman philosopher Seneca described the outer appearance of people in distress:

- a countenance as pale as ashes or as red as blood
- a glaring eye
- a wrinkled brow
- hands restless and perpetually in action, wringing, or menacing
- snapping of the joints
- violent motions of the arms
- stamping of the feet
- trembling lips
- hair standing on end
- a forced, squeaking voice

- broken, deep, and frequent sighs
- ghastly looks, swollen veins
- knocking knees
- rapid heartbeat

When we observe these symptoms in others, we should suspect that they are experiencing a threat to their self-esteem and are in danger of moving from stress to distress.

Detection should always lead to attempts to stop the movement from stress to distress, whether in ourselves or others, because if nothing is done, things will only get worse. Once begun, the distress process rarely reverses itself without help.

Detainment

Detainment has to do with preventing someone's conflict from getting even worse. There's a continuum that moves from success, to stress, and then to distress. The farther along the continuum, the more the threat to a person's self-esteem. While being in stress is frustrating, it's also invigorating, and problem solving can be challenging. However, once the line between stress and distress has been crossed, the experience ceases to be pleasant or challenging and becomes threatening and desperate. People in distress are fighting to stay alive. Only when they cross back into stress is there any possibility of the situation becoming exciting again. Until then, people will be in great pain and anxiety.

Once across the stress/distress line, the experience isn't always the same. In fact, there's a distress continuum, too. People can be a little, moderately, or greatly distressed. What is bad can get even worse. The goal of detainment is to keep conflict from getting any worse. It's like triage in an emergency room, where the most serious wounds are treated first to keep the patient alive, even if this means other wounds are neglected for a time.

To prevent the experience of distress from becoming even more painful, it's absolutely essential that some space and time be put between the situation and the distressed person. People in conflict must get away from the situation, or they will only go further into conflict. They need a chance to recoup and rethink their predicament, bolster their self-esteem, and calm down. As long as they stay in the distressful situation, their only defense is the combat approach; conventional and Christian attempts to reduce conflict take some breathing room and space. Since the combat way is not the preferred way, it behooves anyone in charge of such a situation to arrange a break in the proceedings to allow the return of reason.

Declaration

When people declare something, they announce it to the world. The key to using declaration to prevent conflict is in its timing. It won't work once you're in conflict. It only works if you have a plan of action thought out in advance, which you can put into operation when conflict seems to be inevitable.

I've consulted with several churches with members who had gone into conflict. After we take a number of steps to reduce the conflict, I always recommend that they sit down and decide what they would like to do the next time such a situation arises. I recommend that they announce these plans to the congregation and that the pastor preaches them from time to time — long before any trouble arises. A church might declare two things. First, we are going to try to settle our differences as Christians who are loved by God and are attempting to make peace with one another. Second, if and when we see people becoming frustrated, we will stop what we're doing and restore their self-esteem, because people are more important than our differences.

Individuals can do the same thing for themselves, deciding in advance what they'll do the next time they feel a threat to their self-esteem. They can prevent themselves from going into conflict if they have stated a plan of action, shared it with someone else, and written it down somewhere.

The effectiveness of planning how you will act under stress was dramatically illustrated in the Iditarod sled-dog race in Alaska. Susan Butcher was behind for several of the eleven days, but she finished the race fourteen hours ahead of the next team. How? One of the ways she trained for the race was to run her dogs over the last one hundred miles again and again in the days before the race to familiarize them with the terrain of those last miles. When they came to them, they'd know the end was near and keep up their efforts. She planned what she would do when she came to this final tiring section of the race, and it worked; her dogs raced to the finish.

If you plan what you will do when you are in danger of moving from stress to distress, there's a good chance you'll fall into automatic pilot and do what you planned when the time comes.

Through use of deterrence, detection, detainment, and declaration, it's possible to prevent yourself and others from going into conflict when frustration and a damaged self-image make conflict a very real danger. Any effort these techniques may require will be well worth expending, because it will take far more effort to come out of conflict if you allow the situation to get out of control.

14

Pardon Me, Jesus

or

Helping a Friend in Conflict

Country singer John Prine sings a song titled "Everybody Needs Somebody That They Can Talk To." In this song, the singer meets Jesus on a road, sees He's upset about something, and asks what's the matter. Jesus asks the singer to sit down and talk to Him until He feels better. After a little discussion of His problems, Jesus walks out across the water to calm the storm, calling back over His shoulder, "So long. Thanks for listening."

Even though the song is a fantasy, it does point out some important points about how we can help our friends when they're in conflict. Jesus often talked to His closest friends. He asked them to follow Him and stay with Him as friends and disciples (Mark 1:17). He asked them questions (Matthew 16:13), explained His way of teaching to them (Matthew 13:10-16), and warned them of His approaching death (Luke 18:31-33). He comforted them and taught them how to live when He would no longer be physically with them (John 14-16), asked for their help and comfort at Gethsemane (Mark 14:34), and returned to them after His death to tell them what to do next (Mark 16:14-18).

In this way we're all very much like Jesus. We need a friend to talk with when we're upset and in conflict, and we welcome the chance to discuss our problems with others. If you have a friend in conflict, rest assured that your help is wanted, even if your friend can't express that need directly. But what does your conflicted friend need from you? What will help the most, and how do you go about it?

Recognize the Distress

The first step is to recognize the fact that your friend is in distress. The singer in John Prine's song said to Jesus, "Pardon me, Jesus. You look tired." This immediately told Jesus that the singer was aware of His state of mind and willing to be helpful, even though he didn't know exactly what was bothering the Lord.

Real friends know when their friends are upset. They're sensitive to their feelings and aren't afraid to say, "You look terrible! What's wrong?" Casual acquaintances don't do this. Most of the time, acquaintances won't even notice the signs of distress, and if they do, they back away instead of engaging and trying to help. One of the great truths illustrated by the story of the Good Samaritan is that he even saw the man in the ditch and realized he wasn't a drunk, but someone in need of help. Who really looks at the homeless people lining the streets of our cities today? It's safer not to notice, not to make eye contact, and to walk by on the other side of the street. But, friends hear the little catch in a voice, see the touch of red about the eyes, and empathetically know when someone they care for has a problem.

This sensitivity is a skill that has to be learned and practiced. At first we almost have to force ourselves to stop and commit ourselves to helping, because it does leave us vulnerable to rejection and psychological (if not physical) danger. Maybe you really don't feel like getting involved in your neighbor's problems that particular day, maybe your own problems are heavy enough, or maybe you're afraid of a lawsuit. It takes courage and skill to be a good friend.

I once taught under a dean who had the lovely habit of walking into my office unannounced. He'd sit down and ask, "How're you doing?" The look on his face and his informal manner always helped me open up and talk to him. I felt he really cared and wanted to understand my concerns.

It doesn't take much to show people you care for them and want to help — just a sentence or two:

- How're you doing?
- Are things going okay?
- You look upset. Are you all right?
- What's bothering you today?
- I saw your face getting red in there. Do you want to talk about it?

Don't hold back. Ask the question, because people who are feeling deeply threatened want and need someone to talk to.

Listen

Anyone who's ever experienced an earthquake knows the sense of relief that floods over you when the floor stops moving and the walls cease to shake. The broken water pipes may still be flooding your house, but the floor is now firm enough to stand on while you deal with your problems. Things are going to get better from then on, not worse.

Having someone listen to you when you're in distress does the same thing. It doesn't solve your problems, but it does prevent your distress from worsening and hold out hope of recovery.

How does listening work this miracle? John Prine's song gives us a hint when it says, "everybody needs somebody . . . to open up their ears and let that trouble through." Prine may be a better psychologist than he knows, since when people listen to us, they open our ears and let us hear ourselves.

Before that happens, we're only talking to ourselves, stirring ourselves up and making our conflict all that deeper. I can remember driving to work one day while in conflict over the actions of a colleague that had hurt me. I talked to myself, rehearsing what I was going to say when I got the chance. Anger and hatred welled up in me as I muttered to myself and planned my revenge. I wasn't doing myself any good by talking to myself this way — I was only deepening my own conflict.

If I'd had someone else to talk to that morning, my panic would have lessened, my thoughts and words would have been less passionate and more measured. I would have heard what I was saying, realized how silly I sounded, and calmed down. I would still have had to deal with my hurt, but I wouldn't have been in a panic about it.

How do you listen to a friend in conflict? Good listeners *empathize* instead of *sympathize*. They try to understand the situation from the viewpoint of the upset person, not from their own positions. Telling upset people that they shouldn't be upset because such a thing wouldn't upset you is useless. It's already upset them, and they don't need you doing more damage to their already fragile self-images by poo-pooing their concerns. Accept the fact that they've been upset by a valid problem, put yourself in their position, and try to get to the root of the problem. Ask questions, draw them out. Be sure you're hearing exactly what they're saying, verbally and emotionally, while you offer comfort and support. Until you know what caused their conflict, you can't help them.

At the same time, you have to avoid becoming part of the problem. Maintain your distance, don't rush in with quick solutions, and don't take over for distressed people. Treat them with dignity and respect by quietly but actively listening at this stage.

Probe Beneath the Issue

Being listened to stops the walls and floors from shaking, giving distressed people a foundation to stand on, but it doesn't solve their problems. Before they can begin to solve their problems, they need insight into them. You can't fix a broken water pipe if you can't see it or hear the water rushing between the walls. Only insight into the problem will produce change and reduce conflict, and this requires a little probing behind the wall.

Once you've listened to your conflicted friends with empathy, they'll believe you care enough to see the situation from their point of view. Only then will they be ready to hear your suggestions.

Probing is based on the belief that things are rarely as they seem, that there's another point of view to every problem. At this point, your conflicted friends are only seeing their side of the issue, and they're seeing that in a distorted form because of their emotional state. You know the problem is deeper and more complex than that, so you need to help your friends realize this. This takes a considerable amount of self-control and tact on your part, but it's something you have to do if you really want to help.

Remember, to a person in conflict, the issue is not the issue. The facts are only part of the story — the tip of the iceberg. What lies beneath the surface is the person's injured self-esteem. Probing goes beneath the tip of the iceberg, explores the true reasons for the conflict, and gives your friends the insight they need to deal with their problems effectively. Once they realize that they're in emotional conflict over the issue and not thinking clearly, they can begin the trip back to reason.

For example, a student once told her friend that a

professor had insulted her in class. "All I did was raise my hand and ask if the economic situation of India during the 1930s was similar to that of South Africa in the 1950s. He looked at me with exasperation and said sarcastically, 'Miss Bowen, had you been in class last Thursday, you would know the answer to that question. Please see me after class.' I was humiliated. To add to it, after class he didn't allow me to give any explanation. He launched into me with accusations about my attendance and my lateness with the last paper. I have never been so mad. He had no right to insult me without listening!"

The issue here is really the student's damaged self-esteem, not the professor insulting her. Had she gotten a better night's sleep, had a good time at a party the night before, or had a friend with her when she saw the professor, she might not have felt insulted or might have calmly promised to be more punctual in the future. As it was, his comments were the straw that broke the camel's back, and she went into conflict. She was overwhelmed with desperate feelings that led her to desperate action. In effect, she *let* the situation move her over the stress/distress line.

If her friend had probed beneath the surface complaint, the student might have come to see that she didn't have to react to the professor's comments by going into conflict. She didn't have to like what he said, but she could have used it as constructive criticism and improved her academic performance. Her friend could have shown her that the professor was acting in her best interests by being frank with her — that to some extent he even cared for her if he tried to shape her up.

Probing facilitates this type of insight and releases people from despair so they can take constructive action.

Guide Toward Action

Probing facilitates insight, but guiding leads to change. Counselors say there is no healing without insight, but insight *doesn't* heal. What does heal? Action. Action heals, changes things, and reduces conflict. Guidance provides the basis for action.

Sometimes friends think they shouldn't give guidance. In an old "Peanuts" comic strip, Lucy said to Charlie Brown, "The trouble with you is you're you!"

Charlie Brown was silent. Finally he asked, "Well, what am I going to do about that?"

"Heavens, I don't know!" Lucy answered. "I don't treat, I just diagnose."

This isn't the kind of help people in conflict need from their friends! People in conflict are not being rational. They're thinking is narrow and desperate. Alternatives that they might normally consider aren't even thought of, or are rejected. Once they have gained a little insight into the real issues, they need help in thinking through their options and deciding on a plan of action. In this case, two heads are definitely better than one.

Research into experimental neurosis in rats illustrates this need for guidance. Researchers taught rats to jump toward doors that had cheese behind them. The rats were able to learn that the cheese would always be behind the red door. They were also able to learn that the cheese would be behind the door on the right, regardless of the door's color. They also learned that the cheese would be behind first the red, then the blue door, regardless of which side the door was on.

However, when the researchers shocked the feet of the rats just before they jumped, they began to lose their mastery of the problems and make mistakes. As the shocks continued, the rats narrowed their choice to one door, always jumping to the door on the right, regardless of whether they should choose a certain color, a certain side, or a certain sequence.

People feeling the distress of conflict are like those rats. They lock in one way to get out of their despair. Even when they gain insight through probing, they still feel desperate and need help in getting out of their dilemma. In their minds, only a few actions are possible.

This is where your guidance comes in. Friends willing to take the time to stay with conflicted people can guide them as they think through their options. Charlie Brown asked a good question of Lucy: "Well, what am I going to do about that?" Had Lucy been a sensitive friend, she might have said, "Well, I don't know right off, but I'm willing to think it through with you. Let's put our heads together and see what we can do."

Listening could be summed up as, "Put your head on my shoulder and tell me all about it." Probing could be summed up as, "Let's look at this thing from several points of view. Have you ever thought of it as . . . ?" Guidance could be summed up as, "Let's get three pieces of paper and list your alternatives." This sounds more pedantic than it really is, and it's what your friend needs to calm down and become reasonable. It's not the same thing as denial — saying that what happened wasn't important to your friend — because it was. Guidance simply means dealing with first things first, and getting out of conflict is the first thing that needs to be done.

Right now, you need to help your conflicted friends brainstorm all the actions that could make them feel better — more secure, less upset, more composed, less anxious. *Brainstorming* means considering every possibility, no matter how bizarre it might seem at first. Write each possibility down, whether it seems feasible or not. You'll have a few laughs at some of the wilder ones, but that's good, too. Don't evaluate anything at this point; just come up with every idea you can and write them all down.

When you run out of ideas, go back through your list and evaluate each entry. Would it make your friend feel better? Could it be carried out? Be hard-nosed and logical at this point, whether you're evaluating combat, conventional, or Christian options. Don't forget that some options may work in the short term but lead to further conflict later.

If you do a good job of guiding your friends this way, they should end up with a workable plan that will get them out of conflict.

Support the Plan

The final step in helping your friends out of conflict is to support the plan they've decided on with your help. You are not responsible for doing anything in the plan yourself. Your job is just to stand by your friends as they work their way back to rationality.

People in conflict know they need support. They're scared, anxious, angry, defensive, and insecure. Their plan may look great on paper, but it won't be easy to carry out. Stand firm in refusing to do their work for them, but be lavish and free with your promises of support:

- I'll go with you.
- I'll help you write that letter.
- Call me after you talk with them.
- Call me if you get scared.

These promises of support really work!

The core of support is your availability. Most people can bring themselves out of conflict if they have enough support, but they have to be able to count on it. Being supportive takes time, energy, and commitment on your part, no matter how late in the evening your friends call for it.

Using these steps, you can help your friends out of conflict. There are, however, two cautions. First, there are no guarantees. We humans are fragile; we fall into conflict very easily, and even the best laid plans sometimes fail to work the way they should. Second, it's almost impossible to help if you're the person responsible for the conflict in the first place, especially if you're in conflict yourself. If that's the case, you'll have to work yourself out of conflict before you can go to your friend and try to help. You'll also have to ask for forgiveness for putting your friends into conflict before you can be of help to them. It's not easy being a good friend, but you can be of immeasurable service if you're willing to put yourself on the line.

15

The Forest Greens vs. the Hunter Greens

or

Helping Groups in Conflict

Helping groups in conflict is similar in some ways to helping an individual, but in other ways, it's more difficult and complicated. Something happens when people get together and share the same perception of what's happened. Groups seem to take on a life of their own that can be frightening and overwhelming.

One of the first to recognize this was Thomas Hobbes in his book *Leviathan*. On the cover was a picture of what seemed to be a huge giant. Closer examination revealed that the face, arms, and torso of the giant were all made up of little people grouped together. Hobbes's book was about the gargantuan strength of people who have a "common mind." This common mind means that when a group's self-esteem is threatened, its members protect themselves by agreeing to see the world the same way. They unconsciously block off other points of view and speak in unison about what happened and what must be done. This tendency makes helping groups out of conflict much more difficult than helping individuals.

A church I know of illustrates this very well. Soon after a new minister came to the church, he attended a meeting where painting the fellowship hall was being discussed. He was puzzled when he heard impassioned speeches being made in behalf of *forest* green and *hunter* green—both of which looked the same to him. Emotions ran high, voices were raised, and much mumbling was going on. When the vote was taken, it was a tie, so the chairman wisely put the issue off for another meeting.

For a full year, the forest green proponents and the hunter green proponents opposed each other on almost every decision that came before the church. They differed on whether to have special services, who to invite for the yearly revival, when to hold vacation church school, whether to hire a choir director. Only at the beginning of his second year did the pastor learn what lay behind their animosity toward one another.

Ten years before, a son in one of the families had been a high school sweetheart of a daughter in another of the families. They planned to get married after graduation, but he received a sports scholarship to a university. He then decided to put off the marriage for a year, saying he would take his new bride back to college with him at the start of his sophomore year. However, during his year away he fell in love with another young woman and broke off the engagement to his high school sweetheart.

The family of the girl never forgave him. They and their friends at church transferred their pain and anger to the family of the boy. As the years went on, the animosity and alienation grew, until by the time the new minister arrived, the sides were set. They didn't like each other, and their unified way of looking at things made them oppose almost everything the other group proposed. Helping these two groups out of conflict would be a much more difficult task than helping one of them individually.

Gustav LeBon, an early twentieth-century French thinker, gave a rationale for what happens to groups in his book *The Crowd*. He said that when groups of people come together around a case, they lose their minds and are governed entirely by their feelings. This transition from reason to emotion is the very essence of going into conflict. According to LeBon, crowds are irrational and driven entirely by their feelings, which are always desperate and drastic. Lynch mobs and riotous group protests are examples of this. Convincing crowds or mobs that they can come out of conflict is a difficult job because of the sheer number of individuals involved and because people don't always respond in the same way to any offered help.

Although helping groups out of conflict is difficult, it's not impossible, and those who want to help shouldn't be scared away. The Christian Conciliation Service provides helpful guidelines for working with groups, particularly groups such as the church in the preceding illustration.

Assume the Role

The first step in helping groups come out of conflict is to assume that you have a right to help. You can't be timid or cautious in this role and still be effective. When lawyers in the Christian Conciliation Service discover they have Christians for clients, they take the initiative and encourage the plaintiff and defendant to settle their dispute out of court. They boldly assume the role of mediators and ask their clients to let them intervene in the controversy.

Anyone who wants to help groups reduce their conflicts must do the same thing. Boldly assume the role of mediator and forthrightly ask the hostile groups to let them intervene. This can be done by almost anyone determined to bring a group out of conflict.

I recently heard a good example of just how this can be done. Two Little League teams where playing in the quarterfinals of the playoffs when there was a controversial call by an umpire in the ninth inning that resulted in one of the teams wining the game. A number of the parents on the losing team protested loudly, but the umpire wouldn't change his mind. Several of the parents convinced the losing coach to lodge a protest with the league officials. At the meeting that followed, the coach and parents presented their case in a firm, demanding manner. The other umpires and the rest of the coaches joined in defending the umpire's call. Both sides became louder and louder.

It was obvious to one of the coaches that both groups were distressed and going into conflict, so he stood up and said, "If you will all be quiet, I have something to say." Then he continued, "I've observed us for the last hour. We started out well, but we've gotten more and more upset. I don't think we're getting anywhere, and if we continue like this, we'll end up with deeply hurt feelings. I'm wondering if you would let me lead us in a process that I think will calm us down and let us be reasonable with each other again?"

Somewhat begrudgingly, they all agreed, and he started a process that did just what he said it would do. Because of this coach, they weathered a storm that could have turned into a hurricane. Many times groups continue in conflict because no one stands up and says, "Wait a minute. We need to stop what we're doing and approach this situation another way. I think I can help us do that, if you'll let me." Someone has to assume the role of a helper when groups are in conflict.

Assume Unity of Purpose

The first thing someone assuming the role of helper must do is make both sides of the groups in conflict admit that they have the same purpose. This sounds more complicated than it really is. Suppose the new pastor of the divided church had assumed the role of helping them out of conflict. He could have forced them to reflect on their common purpose. Had they been asked to stop and think about their real goal, they all would have said, "To make this a better church." The pastor then could have said, "Good. We're all Christians here. Although we might differ on the way to do it, we're all interested in making this a better church. There's no one here who doesn't have the best interest of the church in mind. Do you agree with me on this?" Few members of either group would disagree with this statement.

Assuming a common purpose rarely deals with the real issue, though. In the case of the divided church, the real issue was the humiliation that one family experienced at the hands of another. Assuming a common purpose focuses on the immediate issue, not the root problem. Not that the past is unimportant, but where groups are concerned, going to the core of the problem often provokes more trouble than it's worth.

Clarify the Differences

Clarifying the differences is similar to listening when trying to help a friend, with one significant difference: When working with groups, the emphasis is always on the issues rather than the feelings. In fact, when clarifying the differences, everyone should be forced to stick to the facts of the case and not be allowed to drift into accusations or blaming. The idea is to stick to the issues and avoid personalities.

It is helpful to write the issues on a blackboard so everyone can see what's dividing the groups, refining the statements until both sides agree that these are the opinions separating them. Clarifying the issues clears the air of all extraneous feelings — at least on the surface. There will still be issues beneath the surface, and these are really the major issues, because they have to do with self-esteem. But, in dealing with groups, helpers should focus on solving the problem first and dealing with feelings second. Solving the problem in a way that's satisfying to both groups will go a long way toward reducing the anxiety and threat felt by individual members.

Decide on a Solution

Deciding on a solution doesn't mean solving the problem. It just means coming to an agreement on the *type* of solution that will satisfy both sides. The helper should assist the group to find a type of solution that would leave each side feeling it had not been defeated — not a type of solution that would leave each side feeling they had won. In a situation such as this, both sides rarely win, but both sides need not lose.

If helpers can get both sides to say, "We'll find a solution that doesn't force either side to admit defeat," the groundwork is laid for them to work together reasonably. This step is designed to let the two groups find a compromise that doesn't force either of them into a loser's corner.

Encourage Regrets

Some people think that clarifying the differences and deciding on a solution should naturally lead to attempts to find a solution, but this intermediate step actually encourages regrets by helping group members probe beneath the surface to explore the ill will between them. Encouraging regrets is based on the fact that problems are different from conflicts. People in conflict have experienced desperate feelings that led to drastic actions. They crossed the line between stress and distress, and distress involves feelings that are brittle, devastating, and rejecting. These people have gone from caring about the issues to discounting the value of other people.

Encouraging regrets paves the way for good problem solving. Without admitting these feelings about others, solutions to the problem will be contaminated and confounded. One of the goals of helping groups out of conflict is to enable them to go back to the problem and solve it without hard feelings. Encouraging regrets makes this possible.

Encouraging regrets requires skill — sensitive skill. Although group members will feel hopeful because the issues have been clarified and the type of solution has been agreed on, they might be reluctant to admit that they have had ill will toward the other group's members. The helper may want to make ill will normal by saying, "When people feel strongly about an issue, it's quite common for them to personalize the issues and think members of the other group are terribly misguided, evil, and ill-intentioned. I suspect we've felt that way in this controversy. Before we can go on to solve our dispute, I suggest we close our eyes and reflect on the anger and wrath we've felt toward one another."

In Christian groups this can lead to repentance and forgiveness. In secular ones, it can lead to regrets and a commitment to work together without suspicion or hostility. In either case, encouraging regrets about wrath and ill will provides a firm foundation for the final step in helping groups out of conflict.

Reconsider the Problem

The last step in helping groups out of conflict is to lead them in reaching a solution to the problem over which they went into conflict. In the case of the divided church, the old hurts may never fully heal. However, if someone could help them become civil to one another, they could reconsider their opinions and reach a solution that didn't offend either group. Perhaps one group could decide on the color of the walls while the other decided who would be the new church-school superintendent.

Helpers must be trustworthy and highly persuasive. To be effective, the helper must be seen by the groups in conflict as someone who is genuinely motivated to help them get beyond the impasse of their anxious, angry emotions. A helper must also be a sensitive risk taker, especially willing to become involved — and stay involved until the successful resolution of the conflict.

Conclusion

So, what can one do when getting along seems impossible? The answer is "Reduce conflict!" This may seem like a trite answer to a serious and complex problem. But reducing conflict is not an easy task. Nevertheless, reducing conflict is feasible, as this book has, I hope, demonstrated.

Although I suggested that it is possible to live life without going into conflict, it is highly improbable. In fact, I concluded that we all go into conflict at some time or other. Conflict is inevitable. Therefore, learning how to reduce conflict is a necessary skill — both for our own mental health and for getting along with other people.

Skills can be learned. We are all born with the ability to learn how to reduce conflict. Whether we learn to do so is up to each one of us. We can't blame anyone else except ourselves if we fail. We can acquire the skill to get along when getting along seems impossible — if we master the ideas in these pages and diligently practice them.

Let me briefly summarize them.

First, we should remember that there is a radical difference between problems and conflict. Problems are differences of opinion. Conflicts are threats to our self-esteem.

Second, we should look inside ourselves and identify what happens when we go into conflict. We should, also, become sensitive to the way other people act when their self-esteem is threatened. These insights give us cues which make it possible for us to stop conflict when it arises and prevent it before it gets out of hand.

Third, we should become aware of the several methods humans use to reduce the conflict in themselves. Knowing the processes involved in combat, conventional, and Christian ways to reduce conflict will provide helps for us as we attempt to understand ourselves and relate creatively to other persons.

Finally, we should develop well-thought-out plans for handling conflict when — even before — it arises. Although we cannot always be successful in reducing conflict so that problems can be solved, we can try to do our best. As the old maxim states, "Something happens to the best laid plans of mice and men." But we will be far better off in getting along when getting along seems impossible if we have thought ahead about what will work and what is best.

No author every fully succeeds in his goals. Nevertheless, if the ideas I have shared in this book carry us but one step closer to becoming the peacemakers about whom Jesus spoke in the Sermon on the Mount, I will consider my efforts fulfilled. So may it be.